Édouard Glissant

The Baton Rouge Interviews
with Alexandre Leupin

THE GLISSANT TRANSLATION PROJECT

Édouard Glissant

The Baton Rouge Interviews

with Alexandre Leupin

translated by
Kate M. Cooper

LIVERPOOL UNIVERSITY PRESS

LES ENTRETIENS DE BATON ROUGE
avec Alexandre Leupin
© Editions Gallimard, 2008

First published 2020 by
Liverpool University Press
4 Cambridge Street
Liverpool
L69 7ZU

Copyright © 2020 Liverpool University Press

The right of Kate M. Cooper to be identified as the editor of this book has been asserted by her in accordance with the Copyright, Designs and Patents Act 1988.

All rights reserved. No part of this book may be reproduced, stored in a retrieval system, or transmitted, in any form or by any means, electronic, mechanical, photocopying, recording, or otherwise, without the prior written permission of the publisher.

British Library Cataloguing-in-Publication data
A British Library CIP record is available

ISBN 978-1-78962-096-2 cased
ISBN 978-1-78962-130-3 limp

Typeset by Carnegie Book Production, Lancaster
Printed and bound by CPI Group (UK) Ltd, Croydon CR0 4YY

Key Signs and Key Things:
An Introduction to Édouard Glissant's Essays

Entering Glissant's works is to discover a new world, in which many of our assumptions are challenged: first, concerning our material and natural environment and second, regarding philosophy, criticism, theory and thought. Glissant is indeed one of those very rare individuals, an original thinker. Although in his early years he followed a classic university curriculum in philosophy, ethnology, literature and history at the Université de la Sorbonne, ultimately resulting in a Master's degree, he never abandoned a dual vision rooted in his formative years spent in the former French colony of Martinique and, later on, in his contact with European culture. His thought is therefore a hybridization of these two backgrounds, a mixing that he will maintain, elaborate and develop beyond those two mainstays all his life long, while keeping a critical distance with respect to those two constitutive spaces.

This will allow him to escape the pitfalls of academic silos, of misleading universals, of closed systems of thought, of critical ghettos, of identity politics, of the reduction of poetry and thought to ideology. All these tenets are regularly contested by Édouard Glissant. He also rejects labels like Francophonie, postmodernism and postcolonialism. As a matter of fact, his thinking sets aside all determinations and constraints, 'even those that he has formulated *for himself*' (this volume, p. 20), to open itself to a radical freedom. It calls for its readers to open a space of listening beyond their own prejudices, assumptions and presuppositions.

He thus positions himself freely and independently outside the current state of academic criticism, which, in the humanities tends to produce an infinite fragmentation of disciplines and subfields that ignore each other and don't talk to each other: a hermetic and hermeneutic obscurantism that obliterates beauty and literature. All disciplines, all manifestation of art and beauty, contribute to the development of his thought.

Glissant's reader should always keep in mind that his primary means of expression, which supersedes all others, is poetry, whether it manifest itself in novels, plays, poems or essays. He eschews the abstract dryness of customary philosophical prose and thus shows his affinity with the pre-Socratics, the first philosophers, who wrote the first treatises on nature in verse. Glissant's thought is always open to the power of a rich imaginary and imagery which is consubstantial with all his writings, whatever their genres.

Glissant proposes a thinking of general blending, not only of notions, but of material objects, including the materiality of poetry. Hence, for example, in the present book, the great Western epics (the *Aeneid*, the *Song of Roland*) will be put into dialogue with the epics of Latin America (the *Popol Vuh* and the *Chilam Balam*). In *La cohée du Lamentin*, the stallion from the Lascaux cave (15,000 BCE) is placed side by side with Uccello's chivalric mounts (fifteenth century) and the dying horse in Picasso's *Guernica* (1937). These relations between cultural objects don't transcend space and time, since they are considered in their materiality and historical origins; rather, they are contrasted and synthetized in their material copresence in our imaginary.

I said that Glissant was an original thinker. These examples show, however, that his uniqueness does not reside upon a *tabula rasa*. Quite to the contrary, his thinking is built upon the entirety of human history and culture: this past is not restricted to a specific region or time, and boundaries are shattered. In addition, everything past is submitted to what he calls 'the prophetic vision of the past': he looks on history for what could shape and inspire the future, hence producing a reinterpretation of our diverse histories. Hegel's Minerva Owl, which took flight at dusk to enlighten the obscurities of past philosophical thinking, can also, in Glissant's work, fly away at dawn, towards a future of endless possibilities. There is no immutable fixity, even the past changes, we can find in long past cultures signs that have been repressed, forgotten or occulted and that may presage unforeseen futures.

While Glissant adopts the process of Hegelian dialectics, he rejects the philosopher's Absolute Knowledge, by which man, thought and history come to definitive synthesis and closure in Hegel. Such is his dictum: when Western History comes to an end, histories begin.

Let us now review some of the major notions at work in Glissant's thought at work in essays his as well as in his creations, which cannot be separated: poetry thinks, and 'philosophy is an art'. In order to clarify things, we need to isolate them somewhat artificially, while being aware that Glissant's work is a unified, immense, and evolving flux, where everything is organically linked to everything.

In opposition to root-identity, supposedly closed upon itself and excluding those who do not partake in its blood or cultural genealogy, Glissant proposes *relation-identity*, which is defined by the exchanges, not only between individuals, but also between cultures: 'I change, by exchange with the other, without losing myself or denaturing myself'. Identity is thus not immovable, it is submitted to change by the exchange with others, without being absorbed and erased by otherness. In brief, obliquely, through detours (which is an element of his poetics), he practices a conceptualization of identity that differs radically from identity politics and its related literary theory. Glissantian identity does not hark back, in a reactionary fashion, to root identity (or identity defined by prejudice), but on the contrary opens the way for future and unending redefinitions.

Identity raises the question of filiation and origins; in Glissant's vision, there is no pure origin, a One from which everything would derive. This can be verified at the level of genetics, but also as far as cultural geneses are concerned. It is not only Caribbean cultures that are born from diverse civilizational strands, but also Western cultures, which emerged from historical, dialectical struggles, for example the battle between the Greco–Roman heritage and Catholicism. Culture is thus always the result of a *digenesis*. This applies also to abstract theories and critical inquiry, which reduce complexity through a unifying coherence, hence discarding differences.

Glissant is aware of the present intermingling of cultures and people, immeasurably quickened today by the internet and globalization. However, he found the inspiration for his notion of *creolization* in the rapid advent of creole languages, ushered in by colonization and slavery. Creolization designates the interpenetrations of cultures, defining the state of the present world. It is thus for Glissant the preeminent sign of modernity, which make of our times a *globality* to be distinguished from economic *globalization*, which has, after all, no cultural ambition. If we practice the prophetic vision of the past, we can readily see that creolization was a major factor in the emergence of European cultures, which were built upon the remnants of Roman colonies. Hence, Glissant's affinity with the Middle Ages, which he studied at the Sorbonne, and which gave me, as a medievalist, the idea of the interviews that led to the publication of the present book.

Globality lends itself to a pondering of totality, even if we are in an age deeply suspicious of the concept because of its association with the totalitarianisms, left and right, of the twentieth century, and their millions of victims. But Glissant's totality is not to be confused with its dystopian manifestations in the last century, first because it is all-inclusive, without, of course, exclusion regarding races, sexes, cultures; second because totalization is by Glissant an open-ended process, welcoming an unpredictable future and ready to consider what will develop. Totalitarianism entails a rigid and exclusionary fixity, whereas Glissantian totality is neither static nor descriptive; it gets rid of any notion of supremacy that was consubstantial with the triumph of the Aryan race or the proletariat and made totality a raw political grab of power. Totality is prospective and open to change and always becoming, which explains that no statement, past or present, is definitive. Late in his work, Glissant will name totality the *Whole-World*, which is not only a notion, but the all-encompassing weighting of things, down to the most minute material details, from the past and the present, from nature and culture.

Glissant's master notion is without a doubt *Relation*. It appears indirectly in his first essay, *Soleil de la conscience*, published in 1956, and then will accompany every stage of the concrescence of his works. Relation is not to be confused with or confined to the relationship of an Ego to another, or of a group to another, since it has a truly limitless extension and potential for application. As Jacques Coursil states, 'Relation has no outside'.*

Over the years, Glissant expressed Relation in different ways, but some elements of the definition have remained stable. This permanent core I name a *logion*, a self-explanatory statement that is at once central to thought and not subject; Glissant's logia are not catchphrases to be recited with an incantatory tone, but crystallizations of thoughts that have been meticulously pondered and thus beg for active interpretations. They are prods for our thinking.

In the following schema, the Relation *logion* is highlighted by a text box.

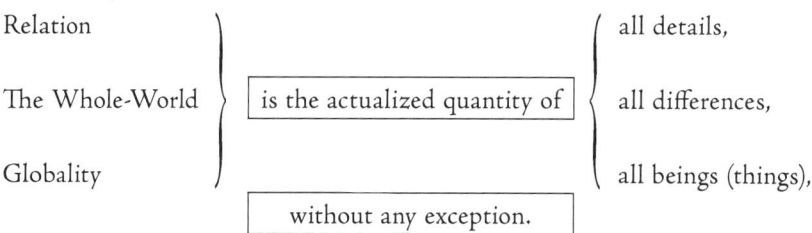

'Actualized quantity' is carefully pondered to designate material things in the world (words, poetry and thoughts included). As such, Relation

---

* 'La Catégorie de la relation dans les essais d'Édouard Glissant, philosophie d'une poétique', in Jacques Chevrier, dir., *Poétiques d'Édouard Glissant* (Paris: Presses de l'université de Paris-Sorbonne, 1999), http://www.edouardglissant.fr/coursil.pdf.

marks a rupture with metaphysics and ontology, which, from Plato and Aristotle through Heidegger, focuses on Being as an abstraction from material reality. Being designates the abstract essence of things (beings) and *qualities* are added to it (like time, place, colour, etc.). Glissant's thought instead posits quantity at its core, meaning 'material things in the world' (*étants* in French, *beings* in English).

'Without any exception' denotes the totalizing aspect of Glissant's thinking: nothing is excluded, Relation can be applied to everything. It is thus closely related to the Whole-World, past, present and future.

The 'unstable' elements (Relation, the Whole-World, globality; details, differences, beings) are variants that are commutable and substitutable: they are hence approximate synonyms which induce, at any moment, a different angle to the core of the definition. The use of certain elements depends on their pertinence to the moment they are uttered, what the Sophists, whom Glissant admired, called the *kairos*. The interplay of these combinations indicates that there is no hierarchy between the notions, no primary elements or principles upon which other notions depend and from which they can be derived. As he states in the interviews: 'Relation has only Relation principles'.

Allow me to give two examples extracted from the present volume.

First, an apparent tautology, a serpent which bites its tail: 'Relation is unnamable. Why? Because it cannot be named'. This tautology is resolved by Glissant's own answer: Relation cannot be named, i.e. given a definitive, conceptual form, 'because it is unpredictable'. Relation is open to the future, a future still unknown to us. Hence, naming Relation is always too early, because it is an endless process of becoming whose figure we don't know in our present.

Second, an axiom: 'Relation is not a happy ending [*un bon devenir*]'. Here, Glissant at the same time follows and dissociates himself from Hegelian dialectics. For Hegel, there was a happy ending to the historical process, Absolute Knowledge, when, his task done, the philosopher could return to the serene contemplation of nature. But, as we know and as Glissant emphasizes, historical dialectics are never-ending. Even as Western History comes to a close, different histories emerge elsewhere. That means that Hegelian negativity, which contradicts the initial thesis, is still at work. Relation doesn't prejudge negativity, doesn't moralize it, since it has a crucial role to play in the emergence of future positivenesses, whose forms we cannot fathom. Hence this statement that was made during an interview: 'Relation has no morality'.

In other words, the final synthesis is always to be construed. Relation cannot ever morally prejudge what will happen.

Édouard Glissant's thought is a radical transmutation of all thought and all human culture; it soars beyond our horizons, meticulously extracted from what has been thought from the origin of thinking to the present day; beyond the One and the Heraclitean Logos (through the multiple copresence of all languages), beyond the Parmenidian and Heideggerian Being (through the consideration of the variety of *beings*), beyond singular identity (through relations between communities), beyond all universals, be they Catholic or philosophical, beyond the Hegelian system (through the poetic imaginaries of future histories), beyond the academic discourse (through the unpredictability of becoming), beyond filiations and cultural traditions (through the meticulous and prophetic re-reading of the past, which becomes an exciting future in its incompleteness); it is a flight beyond the partly illusory mastery that philosophy, science, theory usually tend to impose on beings.

Glissant's works, which consider all causalities and all determinisms to, in the end, overcome them, open all cultures to an abyssal and exalting freedom, not without its frights – the 'thought of trembling' perhaps:

The power of imaginaries is an everyday utopia, it is realistic when it prefigures what will allow for a long time to accompany actions that do not tremble. Actions that do not tremble would remain sterile if the thought of world totality, which is trembling, did not support them. This is where philosophy is applied, and also the poem's thought. (*Philosophie de la Relation*, 2009, p. 56)

The critical rereading of all constraints does not lead to a new domination or a vague, shapeless anarchy, but, if I may in turn allow myself an oxymoron, a non-masterly mastery.

This is Édouard Glissant's message: to teach us to live poetically in an unlimited freedom and in the responsibility due to the *Other of thought* (that is, beings in the world that cannot be framed by the abstraction of thought); to open us to the future of an unpredictable becoming, where the essential contours of Relation and the Whole-World are already beginning to be drawn and anticipated.

For a more detailed interpretation of Glissant's thought, see my *Édouard Glissant, philosophe, Héraclite et Hegel dans le Tout-Monde* (Hermann, 2016), a translation of which will soon be published by the State University of New York Press in their series 'Contemporary French Thought'.

A Timeline for Édouard Glissant

21 September 1928	Édouard Godard is born in the Morne Bezaudin, Martinique.
1935–1939	Primary school, Le Lamentin, Martinique.
1938	Édouard Godard is recognized by his father and becomes Édouard Glissant.
1939–1945	High school.
1944	Glissant founds and directs a journal, *Franc Jeu*.
1946	He leaves Martinique to study ethnology and philosophy (under the philosopher Jean Wahl) in France, at the Université de la Sorbonne.
1948	Publication of Glissant's first poems in the journal *Les temps modernes*, founded by Jean-Paul Sartre and Simone de Beauvoir.
1950	Glissant marries Yvonne Suvélor in Paris. He collaborates with the journal *Présence africaine*.
1952	He receives a Master of Arts in Philosophy. His thesis, under Gaston Bachelard's direction, is entiled *Découverte et conception du monde dans la poésie contemporaine*.
1953	Glissant contributes to the journal *Les Lettres nouvelles*, founded by Maurice Nadeau and Maurice Saillet. *Un champ d'îles* (poems) (Paris, Instance).
1955	*La terre inquiète* (poems) (Paris, éditions du Dragon).
1956	*Les Indes* (poem) (Paris, Le Seuil). *Soleil de la conscience, Poétique I* (essays) (Paris, Le Seuil). Glissant participates in the first congress of black writers and artists in Paris.

1958	*La Lézarde* (novel) (Paris, Le Seuil), which receives the Théophraste Renaudot Prize.
1959	Glissant participates in the second congress of black writers and artists in Rome.
1960	*Le sel noir* (poems) (Paris, Le Seuil). Glissant participates in the FAGA (Front Antillo-Guyanais pour l'Autonomie). He signs the *Manifeste des 121* or *Declaration on the right of insubordination in the Algerian War*.
1961	*Le sang rivé* (poems) (Paris, Le Seuil). Visit to Cuba. Glissant is forbidden to stay in Martinique and assigned to reside in Metropolitan France, as one of the leaders of Antillean separatism.
1964	*Le Quatrième Siècle* (novel) (Paris, Le Seuil). Glissant marries Jacqueline Marie Amélie Hospice in Paris.
1965	Glissant is allowed to return to Martinique.
1967	He creates the *Institut Martiniquais d'Études* (IME), a private school, where many artists and writers will be taught.
1969	*L'Intention poétique, Poétique II* (essays) (Paris, Le Seuil).
1971	Glissant founds the journal *Acoma*, hosted by the Parisian publisher Maspéro.
1975	*Malemort* (novel), (Paris, Le Seuil).
1978	*Monsieur Toussaint* (theatre play) (Paris, Le Seuil).
1979	*Boises* (poems) (éditions Acoma, Martinique).
1980	He defends his PhD in sociology at the Sorbonne University with *summa cum laude*.
1981	*Le Discours antillais* (essay) (Paris, Le Seuil), based on his PhD. *La case du commandeur* (novel) (Paris, Le Seuil).
1982–1988	Director of the *Courrier de l'Unesco* (journal). Glissant meets Sylvie Sémavoine.
1985	*Pays rêvé, pays réel* (poems) (Paris, Le Seuil).
1987	*Mahogany* (novel) (Paris, Le Seuil).
1988	Glissant is named distinguished professor and director of the Center for French and Francophone Studies at Louisiana State University.

1989	Doctor *honoris causa* from the Collège universitaire de Glendon, University of York, Canada. Wins the Puterbaugh Prize and lectures at the University of Oklahoma, Norman, under the aegis of *World Literature Today*.
1990	Glissant moves from Le Seuil to Gallimard. *Poétique de la Relation, Poétique III* (essay) (Paris, Gallimard). *Discours de Glendon* (essay) (Toronto, editions du GREF). Director of the Caribbean Carbet Prize.
1991	*Fastes* (poems) (Toronto, éditions du GREF).
1993	*Tout-Monde* (novel) (Paris, Gallimard). Glissant is named honorary president of the International Parliament of Writers (Paris), of which he was one of the founding members. He is named doctor *honoris causa* by the University of the West Indies, first in Trinidad, then in Jamaica.
1994	He is named distinguished professor at the City University of New York Graduate Center. *Les Grands Chaos* (poems) (Gallimard, Paris).
1996	*Faulkner, Mississippi* (essay) (Paris Stock). *Poèmes complets, Introduction à une poétique du divers* (essay) (Gallimard, Paris).
1997	*Traité du Tout-Monde, Poétique IV* (Paris, Gallimard).
1998	Glissant marries Sylvie Sémavoine in New Jersey.
1999	*Sartorius. Le roman des Batoutos* (novel) (Paris, Gallimard).
2000	*Le Monde incréé, poétrie* (theatre) (Paris, Gallimard), which includes three plays: *Conte de ce que fut la tragédie d'Askia* (1963) *Parabole d'un moulin de la Martinique* (1975) *La Folie Celat* (1987).
2002	Creation of the Édouard Glissant Prize at the University of Paris-VIII (Vincennes) in collaboration with La maison de l'Amérique latine and, later, the Institut du Tout-Monde.
2003	*Ormerod* (novel) (Paris, Gallimard).

2004	Glissant is named doctor *honoris causa* by the University of Bologna, Italy.
2005	*La Cohée du Lamentin, Poétique V* (essay) (Paris, Gallimard).
2006	*Une nouvelle région du monde, Esthétique I* (essay) (Paris, Gallimard).
	Glissant founds the Institut du Tout-Monde in Paris.
	The French president Jacques Chirac asks for his participation in the founding of a National Center of Slavery.
2007	*La Terre magnétique, les errances de Rapa Nui, l'île de Pâques* (with Sylvie Séma) (Paris, Le Seuil).
	Mémoires des esclavages (Paris, Gallimard).
	Quand les murs tombent. L'identité nationale hors-la-loi? (pamphlet) with Patrick Chamoiseau (Paris, Galaade).
2008	*Les Entretiens de Baton Rouge*, interviews with Alexandre Leupin (Paris, Gallimard).
2009	*Philosophie de la Relation*, Paris, Gallimard.
	L'intraitable beauté du monde, adresse à Barack Obama (pamphlet) (Paris, Galaade).
	Manifeste pour les produits de haute nécessité (pamphlet) (Paris, Galaade).
2010	*10 mai. Mémoires de la traite négrière, de l'esclavage et de leurs abolitions* (essay) (Paris, Galaade).
	La terre, le feu, l'Eau et les Vents, une anthologie de la poésie du Tout-Monde (poetry) (Paris, Galaade).
	L'imaginaire des langues, interviews with Lise Gauvin (Paris, Gallimard).
3 February 2011	Death in Paris.
2015	Glissant's archives are declared a national treasure by the French government and transferred to the National French Library (BNF).

Timeline established with the help of Professors Jean-Pierre Sainton and Raphaël Lauro.

For Sylvie

*'Finding in the world
reasons for its own transformation.'*

Contents

Foreword   1
Itineraries   3
The Interviews   5
Spumes, the Day After   85
The Mangrove Work   89

Foreword

In 1990 and 1991, when Édouard Glissant was living in Baton Rouge, Louisiana, and teaching at Louisiana State University (LSU), we used to meet regularly to converse. From these exchanges, which took place over the course of a year, I have culled the following set of topics in which the poet reviews and explicates several aspects of his thought. The writer's analyses have lost neither spontaneity nor relevance. Responding to the medievalist that I was at the time, he applies medieval poetics, which he considered according to his own particular point of view as a poetics of Relation, to certain trends of ideas that inform our modernity. Fifteen years later, I have added nothing to the text and, with the exception of going into further detail on certain questions, neither has the poet. Most of the viewpoints brought up here have meanwhile been developed in the writings that Édouard Glissant has since published. This fact only increases their interest. We know the author's predilection for repetition, accumulation, recollection – all of which he considers privileged approaches to knowledge, with the obvious and the ordinary entering as elements.

On the global clash of languages, peoples, and cultures; on the emergence of nation-states; on decolonizations; on the question of identity, here is the vibrancy of his thought. This vibrancy consists of poetically entering the symbolic space of present-day globalization, meditating upon its inextricable and inverted forms, then extracting from these forms the figures of lyrical crystallization.

A.L.
2007

Itineraries

1. 'Universality has no language.'
In which is described both the dialogue and the conflict, between the Catholic and the heretic, universality and particularity, during the Middle Ages as well as today.

2. 'The subtlety, or innocent and instinctive artfulness, of the poet.'
In which the poet's relation to his landscapes is expressed, and the cleaved forms that mark his student years in Paris are defined.

3. 'The aim of writing is not to incite political action.'
In which the poetic necessity of escaping simplified reproduction of political action is articulated, and the mimetic orthodoxies of decolonization are criticized.

4. 'A variegated pattern of transformations … : on the epic.'
In which we discuss the birth of nation-states beginning with the epic impulse, specifically in The Song of Roland, as well as the differences that mark our present in relation to the western Middle Ages.

5. 'Revealing the constants of global Relation.'
In which is expressed the non-imperial imperative for the modern-day poet to engage in the infinite globalness of the inexpressible Relation.

6. 'Separating from the place of speech, the better to return to it.'
In which the poet is called upon to transcend the restrictive circumstances of utterances, and to become involved with the drift of the Whole-World.

7. 'The writer of today is always a future writer.'
In which the future portended by literature is discussed, in a world dominated by the copresence of everything to everything.

8. 'Infinitely multiplying the existence of languages.'
In which we understand that it is not only a question of preserving each of the world's languages, but also of casting each language into the unrepresentable space of its relation to all other languages.

The Interviews

✦ 1 ✦

'Universality has no language'

Édouard Glissant. I would like to suggest this: it would be advisable for us to speak as well with silences. You will surely agree that it would not be a good idea for us to imagine the continuation of our exchange from one sole perspective. Concerning the Middle Ages in the Western World, which you have invited me to consider, can we really claim that there is such a thing as the French Middle Ages? The English Middle Ages? The German or Italian Middle Ages? The idea of nationhood didn't yet exist, and nations were not yet emerging. It is a commonplace to suggest that this period was characterized by a looser, less enmeshed unity. In the same vein, can we speak about the aims of writing and culture during the Middle Ages, as we can during the Classical period or during the Enlightenment? Didn't long periods of silence loom between the manifestations of this medieval voice? And don't those silences imply that the medieval era is important and interesting not only because it sizes up what is to follow – what will be called the Renaissance – but primarily, in and of itself, for the fact that it spins its wheels in an absolutely singular dramatics, a process of interchanging desertions, recoveries, affirmations and negations that don't really contradict each other? And will not this process have to ultimately end or break, confronted by an insurmountable choice? This is what interests us.

I see the European Middle Ages, which actually occurs before there are any Europeans, as a sort of drama: the tragedy of a speech outside of any system, gradually taken up and codified in the first developments of Europe's systematic ideas. It is the emergence of heretical and mystical thought, thought that digresses and derails, and which little by little is set, through systematic, rational and generalizing thrusts, in the extraordinary developmental force of these European cultures.

This tragedy recalls for me what so many contemporary cultures, so many abandoned peoples, are living, flattened by the unstoppable development of great systems that seize and dominate the world, systems that have been perfected beyond imagination: technologies, mass advertising, the performing arts – a ready-made model of taste and ideas. And not two opinions of society as in the Middle Ages, but an infinity of oppressions, all in a unilateral direction. The same despondency of mind, which raises unanswered questions. What do you think about this approximation and about such a relationship?

Alexandre Leupin. To be sure, the idea of taking things for themselves, with their internal structures and conflicts, has always seemed primordial to me, whether we're talking about the Middle Ages or the work of Édouard Glissant. That is one of the engines of my critical approach. It is true that the Middle Ages are a pan-European phenomenon in that a social structure, feudalism, and an intellectual and religious structure, the Church, cover the entire field of societies beyond all differences. In other words, there are two basic and central institutions.

The idea of these interviews came to me while I was examining the remarks that you have made about creolization and its relation to the Middle Ages. If, for example, we observe the birth of the French language, we find that some conditions are, *mutatis mutandis*, the same as those attending the emergence of creole languages.

É.G. And further, we have on the one hand our contemporary era's conditions of creolization, minus the question of languages, and on the other, in the past, the conditions underlying the appearance of native or regional (there's no other way to designate them) languages which will later become national languages. Without making excessive use of comparisons, what interests me about this issue in the Middle Ages is indeed the emergence of languages, an emergence which can clarify the processes of creolization. And especially, it is the concept of humanity that medieval peoples generally made for themselves before this occurrence, which was more an effect of creative expression than of linguistic structure. The Middle Ages are like a tragic theatre in which we see two orders of ideas or faith confront each other, meet, separate, and sound the clarion of a truly intense and disordered dramatic play: on the one hand, there is the truth of Being finding its way through trembling, or groping, sometimes approximative and occasionally transcendental means, in the full mystical sense; on the other hand, there is the rallying to a systematic generalization, in which the order of universality already appears. A current of thought flows throughout the Middle Ages which is sometimes mystical, sometimes heretical, but always 'beside the point'. At the same time there occurs this second order, a system of reviving reason, which is the order of the orthodox, the order of universality. The Middle Ages seem to me to be a theatre in which these two tensions vie with each other for space on the stage. The thinking of order and system, which is the thinking of universality or orthodoxy, will most certainly prevail over mystical thought, even though it's not really possible to dissociate them. Mystical thought exists in orthodoxy and vice versa, but two large axes, two grand orders of vision nevertheless persist: the drama of their opposition (mysticism and orthodoxy) and the drama of the gradual imposition of universal thought, which is the thought of orthodoxy, of Catholic Christianity. These two dramatic tensions continue until the emergence of *mutually precipitated* divergences that occur with the advent of Protestant religions and onset of the wars of religion, the supreme arena of theological battle (but that is a separate question).

The entire scene of action is set off by this drama, and if, later on, we want to study, discuss, or think about the problem of creolization from the linguistic perspective, and those specificities which will, for example, separate *langue d'oil* from *langue d'oc*, or lead to the appearance of regional languages which will in turn either give rise to national languages or dissolve inside them, then it seems to me that we have to view the scene as dominated by the combat between these two forms, these two conceptual orders of Being in the world: the heretical or mystical order, and the catholic order. Transoceanic populations, people born out of the expansion of the Occident, will be submitted to the law of systematic orders, without suspecting that those same orders had already vanquished decentralized thought. Let's just say it: the processes of creolization will be determined by this fact. Paradoxically, the order of feudalism continues in France until the seventeenth century, until its opposition to Louis XIV: it is a divergent, particular, and heretical order, and the order of the Church increasingly asserts itself as the universal and catholic order in the fullest sense of the term, perhaps to oppose itself to the disorders of the time. During this same century, when the French language achieved its own organic unity, it is the sign of true victory of universality in the realm of Louis XIV. The language of rationality vanquished the creolizations relayed and prolonged by Rabelais, Montaigne, and the poets of the Pléiade, heretical orders entirely forgotten during the Great Century.

A.L. It is difficult to separate order from disorder in a simple dialectic. For example, Saint Bernard* is both a counsellor to popes, and almost a pope himself; he is also a great mystic, and a great craftsman of language. In your work as a whole, it is specifically this composition between an orthodoxy (which I will explain) and a certain heresy (fascinating to me) that, to my way of thinking, endows much of what you write with depth and scope. On the side of an 'orthodox' order, I would situate your classical, philosophical, literary and historical formation, and not only in the somewhat simple-minded sense of 'great erudition' (we are all *cultured*). In your work, there is recognition of this imposed heritage. Therefore, despite your preoccupation with marginality, exclusion, and heresy, there is also an aspiration toward universality that enters into a fascinating dialogue with what you call the heretical order. This heretical order concerns not only the geographical and historic margin of an old Caribbean colony, but also the characters, landscapes, Creoles who enter into the composition, probably in the syntax and certainly in the lexicon of the French language (of languages in general), and who appropriate and dialogue with the other side, the orthodox order.

É.G. You could see it from that standpoint. But when you look at the issue that way, it's from the perspective of another time, ours, already an era in which resolution of the dissociated exists. In other words, in modern thought, at a time when we try to reconcile heresy and universality, the rational and the irrational, and still other antinomies, a lot of history has transpired; orthodox universality (and I'm not speaking of orthodoxy in purely religious terms) has already imposed itself, and then has become dissociated (as, for example, under the assault of diversity thinking). Today, we are living during a time when we are repeatedly beginning something else, always trying to resolve the contradictions of the dissociated.

The dramatic aspect of the Middle Ages was that these two orders, or rather, the order and the disorder ripped apart from each other, in no way envisioned an eventual resolution. At that time, one order had to take precedence over the other, the Regent or Rector over the sorcerer's apprentice (so that the history of the West could unfold in its own universal way). This is what seems important and serious to me. This is why all the dramas of mystical or heretical thinking in the Middle Ages are indeed

---

* St Bernard of Clairvaux (1090–1153) was a French Cistercian monk and mystic. Founder and abbot of the abbey of Clairvaux, he was one of the most influential churchmen of his time.

dramas, meaning that they end badly. According to this model, thought is either devastated, as with the Cathars,* or castrated, as with Abelard,** who was perhaps blamed less for his amorous relations than for his commerce of mind with Heloïse, just as was the case for all the women burned at the stake, up to and including Joan of Arc, and all those who indulged in arcane thinking. More simply, it is thinking reduced to silence, the hollow silences of the Middle Ages. After this point it will be said that the Middle Ages do not recognize the individual, that the self is a creation of succeeding times, that during the Middle Ages a sort of extra-human machine is put in place, the machine of universality. And this machine at that time does not conceive, does not and cannot understand, historically speaking, that there are margins, and that these margins can be inhabited. So, add all of the colouration that you will – eschatology, demonology, and the other divergences that are the very mark of an era's sensibility – and you will understand that *something has not been lost*, that something has been deflected from the relation between these two orders, and that it was necessary for one of these orders, universality, to be generally achieved in the world so that it could in turn be questioned and at least relativized. Today, the only difference is that the order of universality has been obliged to concede that there are margins, and that these margins are inhabited, a fact that it could not and did not need to accept in the thick of the Middle Ages. I see the Middle Ages, not only from the linguistic point of view, which we will take up later, but on a deeper level, as an enormous stage, let's call it pre-occidental, upon which this drama will be enacted. Each person may then wonder: 'But what if the thought of Raymond Lull*** drove and oriented the history of the West and not the thinking of Saint Augustine or Saint Thomas? What would have come of it?' By the same token, we can ask this question: 'What would have happened if Hannibal had conquered and destroyed Rome, as the Romans destroyed Carthage?' The history of the West might have tipped toward Africa, the quintessence of another

---

* The Cathars were a religious sect in Southern France. They flourished in the twelfth century CE when they challenged the authority of the Catholic Church.
** Peter Abelard (1079–1142) was one of the most prominent philosophers and theologians of the twelfth century. His love for, and relationship with, the French nun, writer and scholar Heloïse d'Argenteuil has been widely represented and subject to wide interpretation.
*** Ramon Llull (*c*.1232–*c*.1315) – known in English as Raymond Lully or Raymond Lull – was a mathematician, philosopher and writer from Majorca. He is remembered for writing the first major work of Catalan literature. Lull was a polymath whose work has been influential across a range of fields.

diversity. These questions might be considered otiose from the perspective of historical scholarship, but they are not useless from the standpoint of the situation in which we find ourselves today: does the thinking of universality, which is so magnificently and sumptuously realized in the West, does this thinking, in itself and in its methods, still measure up to the task of giving us openings onto the horizon of the world that we currently inhabit?

Or isn't it necessary, considering the diffracted nature of our world and the impenetrability of its grounds, to return to the drama of the Middle Ages, just as we should return to the pre-Socratic and the spiritualities of African cultures, and dive in once again in order to know what happened between these two arenas – the systematic and the non-systematic – so that we might understand what we have to sort out, and how, in the relations between these two valuations of order and disorder in the world? This is why it is so thrilling to examine the European Middle Ages. But we will learn so much from Asia! And from so many other cultures with native dramas and tragic internal contradictions that we haven't had the opportunity to track, and that haven't known the influence of universal thinking.

Beginning in the Middle Ages, at the same time when catholicity, in its full sense as universality, is actualized as a system or systematic thinking and directs all of western history, this systematic and universal mindset was obliged to come to terms with an aspect of diversity: this was the perspective of languages, from which universal thinking has never been able to extricate itself.

What this means is that one of the great, truly universal values of the time, Latin, or the Latin language as a symbol of all learned discourses, and then of native languages (Indo-European), was gradually creolized and yielded 'Latin' languages (along with the dog-Latin of comic theatre). Universality had to undergo this movement. It is an interesting operation, leading to the following conclusion: universality does not have a universal language. OH! The universal that triumphs as a system is not equal to the task of preserving Latin as one of the universal languages: it is obliged to come to terms with regional languages. Universality composes the diverse! Let's say it: the universal has no language.

A.L. My view of the Middle Ages differs from yours. I see the Middle Ages less as a monolith, in the sense that this universalizing of system produces a process which you know and have described very well, and which is essentially modern: the extension of catholicity as a mindset over the universe of system fabricates its own antibodies, its own heretics. The privileged field in which to see this at work is not so much history, sociology or other disciplines, but rather, literary texts. Literary texts of the Middle Ages play out this drama between universality and heresy. In this sense, I believe that they are very close to a part of what you are suggesting. The formula, 'universality has no language', is extremely compelling. I would say yes and no. The case of native languages is there to prove what you are saying, but on the other hand, Latin still remains all across Europe as a language of power, exchange, as well as intellectual, philosophical, and theological discussion. This seems to me to be one of the radical differences from modernity, in the sense that we no longer have any sort of universal language, except for scientific language. The language of science has replaced Latin as a universal language. On the other hand, clerics promoted (see the edict of the Council of Tours in 813)* languages of the Romance language region, obliging priests to preach in vernacular forms. If the message has the charge of universality, then by principle it must be translated into any and all idioms.

É.G. For you and me, it is reassuring that if I think of the Middle Ages as a drama between two spheres of conception about the world, I don't see this drama operating in a monolithic way. Now, I would indeed say that it is surely the West which has shaped thinking about universality and which, from this initial thrust, has given place to its own heresies and its own drama (otherwise we wouldn't be speaking about the Middle Ages as such an interesting period). But what we need to evaluate – and this is why we have to return to the Middle Ages – is that the West, which constituted and begot its own heresies, only to fight immediately against them, exported into the world nothing more than systematic thought. And it wasn't Latin that served this end, but the dominant languages such as French and English, or today the hegemonic Anglo-American with its indirect universal idioms, such as technological (rather than scientific) language, or the language of capitalistic commerce, in which consumption becomes consummation.

Cultures of rationalization have not exported heretical thought into the world. And that is the big question: if you want to gain insight into this

---

* The Council of Tours in 813 decreed that priests should preach sermons in the vernacular 'rusticam romanam linguam', a form of Vulgar Latin understood by the people, and no longer in classical Latin. This was the first recorded official recognition of an early form of French distinct from Latin and is considered by many to be the date the French language was born.

mindset of the sidelined, the marginal, the *otherwise*, which all of these cultures have begotten through a *backlash* to their own universalizing vocation, and which other cultures have perhaps generated quite naturally, then you just have to rummage on your own through the thinking of the margins or of the heresies themselves. To begin with, you will find these possibly in many of the decentralized cultures that were the objects of colonization. If one is not immersed in European, then Western time, if one is elsewhere, then what is directly received is the export: the thinking or the impetus of the universal. Often when I speak about this expansion of the West, when I say that this sumptuous expansion was also mortal, everyone reprimands me: 'Ah! You are against the West!' Not at all. I am trying to see what was conveyed by exportable quantities after having been generalized through abstraction or sublimation, and it is above all this thinking of universality which is the steward of systems. Western impulse has not *generalized* its own most fertile secretions, its own heretical clay (but is that even possible?). It has not exported, nor will it export them. What interests me in the Middle Ages is to find the movement where these two orders confront each other on the soil of what was to become the geographic and dynamic locus of the West. So it really isn't a question of regretting that this was done instead of that, but of seeing, in these two ways of thinking which were tragic and in which irremediable destinies were played out, how certain approaches could converge in a resolution (of the dissociated), in an alignment with our present-day conceptions, and if this resolution or this alignment are desirable.

A.L. That said, critical thought, secularity, the rule of law, democracy, the idea of abolishing slavery, the rights of man and woman, have all arisen solely and strictly in the Western world. In the end, their exportation will include its own criticism as well as the imperialist structure that frames it. Reflecting upon your own historical situation, as far as I am able to do it, I see you in the margin between a centre that has been constructed through criticism, and another margin, still preserved, which has been excluded from these dynamics.

É.G. We can indeed approach the problem in that way, from the standpoint of the orientation and evolution of an individual thought. But we can also approach it in another manner: we may put the universal mind, proposed and exported by European peoples, not in relation to an individual thinking which would be mine or yours, but in relation to cultures taken globally and which had existed before western intervention. (Meanwhile, let's observe that criticism of slavery was created from the same systematic viewpoint of the rational and the expedient, and particularly when the West *no longer truly needed this system of slavery*, at least in its transatlantic and trans-Saharan forms. We'll add that criticism of colonialism, which was *begotten by the West itself*, was the quartermaster of theories about identity that we shall review shortly.) But let's return to the different kinds of cultures that were prey to colonialism. I cannot forget that I recognize myself in a culture that didn't predate Western intervention, a culture that is a consequence of colonization, or more specifically, a neo-American culture. We may well understand that for a Martinican, an Antillean, or an American, the fact of having been submitted to universal thinking in a global way can explain why he is fully equipped to enter into a critical internal examination of the West. This is because he belongs to a civilization and to cultures that were born out of colonial closure. But if we expand the panorama and stick to looking at how Western thinking has been applied to other cultures which existed before any act of colonization, we become aware that there are almost no collective possibilities for these cultures to be assailed, either benevolently or harmfully (of little importance, as it's obviously both), by the thinking of universality, and at the same time engage in the internal criticisms that the West has formulated for itself. This is where it becomes difficult for those various cultures that we would call whole or secure or radically alien to any disposition of the colonizer. The question crops up: could it be that the very concept of the State, as it has been revealed and excessively applied in most African and Asian countries after decolonization, is one of those systematic conceptions so formally and mimetically inherited from Western universal thinking that none of the available heretical thinking (whether secreted by the West or couched inside the cultures in question) could perturb its schematically imparted and imported infiltration? For cultures globally considered exogenous, the heretical thought of the West has not accompanied in any critical fashion the ravaging expansion of the universal idea, to which they have been submitted. Is it enough that these cultures simply live their own dynamics, without bothering about the rest? No, because the theatre of the world demands from now on that these cultures live their lives and expose themselves at the same time to the spectacular generality of the Chaos world. This is why it is injurious that in certain countries conceptions devised about the State or the nation or the territory are coarsely duplicated conceptions of the colonizer, without the marvellous burgeoning of heresies that accompanied the birth of these conceptions *in the West itself,* and for a long time successfully contested them. Neither do these duplicated conceptions include the radical criticism born out of the ex-centric thinking occurring in these cultures of *elsewhere*, a thinking which has remained without historical effect.

Regarding cultures which have originated in part from the colonial act and which have maintained a relationship of tangency or assimilation with it, we need to ask ourselves the following question: to what degree is the ability to engage *from the inside* in criticism of the western systematic generalization an initiatory force of weakness, or at least, a bearer of uncertainty? Assimilation ravages the individual, who then rationalizes, even if rightfully so. I am then no longer the intrepid observer, but instead, an entire enmeshed country.

Let's think about this: we can know nearly everything about the arcana of the European Middle Ages, if we have the passion or the intuition for it, but we know next to nothing about the spiritual orientation of pre-Islamic kingdoms in present-day Mali. We know all the details of the expeditions that led to the discovery of the sources of the Nile, but, as Cheik Anta Diop has indicated, we cannot figure out anything about the cultural links established between Nubia and Egypt during the time of the first pharaohs. I tremble and I deplore these accumulated findings when they are accompanied in me by so much generalized ignorance about another side. Don't you agree?

A.L. I would add that not only does exportation bear uniquely on the universal system, but also that there is no reckoning nor any consideration of the empirical qualities of the Other. What you call 'the schematically imparted and imported infiltration' has been literally applied. This means, for example, that colonized or postcolonial States have been cut up in an altogether arbitrary way, which has given rise to the problems that we know only too well.

♦ 2 ♦

'The subtlety, or innocent and instinctive artfulness, of the poet'

Alexandre Leupin. Let's leave literature aside for the moment to speak about your biography, following the example of the 'vidas' of the troubadours,* and to expose briefly its status. Troubadour poems are assembled in collections that are never isolated from a biographical context, and from a context that presents the poems in a critical fashion. On the one hand, there are the 'vidas' or the lives, and on the other the 'razos', the textual explication of the poem. Both of these frame, graphically and interpretively, the poems of the *fin'amor* tradition. These collections were constituted in the thirteenth and fourteenth centuries after the poems had been sung and/or written. The lives of the troubadours have nothing to do with biographies as we understand them in the usual sense; instead, they are extracted from the poems themselves. This seems to be a rather naïve operation, completely anti-positivist, in that the poem 'causes' the biography, and not the other way around. But this is actually an extremely profound idea, which amounts to saying that poetry or writing is here the cause of life, and not the inverse as a positivist reading would have it. So I have thought that this approach might be a very fertile one for the study of your biography and your writing.

Édouard Glissant. But there is also another interesting perspective that could, as it happens, be related to the case of the troubadours. This is when the personal biography, the biography of the individual or the poet, is blended or lost, or *composed*, in a biography to be created of a collectivity, in a history that is to be reconstituted or recuperated. Now why would this be interesting? Because this sort of inscription is not always

---

* 'Vida', meaning 'life' in Occitan, is a genre consisting of brief prose biographies of the troubadours.

done with forethought, in a volitional manner. An instinct of participative biography is activated. Moreover, there are cases in which the biography of a collectivity resists, cases in which it is fragmented, obscured or obliterated.

This biography of a collectivity does not rely on precise datings, and it is not caught up in a historical continuum. It is constituted out of a sort of chaotic mass of time. The main point of the writing of the poem will be to explore it and to try to constitute time, to construct this continuum. At this moment, the collective biography, the history that the poem is seeking to re-establish (and which is not a history that can be recounted), can only correspond, not strictly speaking but with poetic suggestion and composition, to individual biography. It's not a question of thinking that the poet or writer has a predetermined life nor that he has a sort of originary vocation which would induce him to live one prescribed event rather than another, in one manner rather than another. But we may just as soon affirm that the project of individual existence follows the course of the quest for collective existence. This is interesting for a number of reasons: first, because it is a question of knowing if one can be lost in this collective existence. In other words, does the individual as an individual, perhaps an end in itself, risk being abolished in this quest for a biography of the collective? This is a commonplace of occidental thought, but murkier from the standpoint of many other cultures. The second point is precisely that the search for continuum in the biography of the collective – in every case where collectivities have been dispossessed of their memory and their histories – the search for what might be called a series of datings, the recapture of time, and further along, a series of 'accounts', is linked to a vision that one makes of history in general as determining each particular history. Now, what I believe is that every individual and every poet, particularly in his or her biography, expresses a certain conception or vision of history. And I have almost always had a presentiment of this notion of history, and so have tried to formulate it in terms that would conceptually escape from the way that History is envisioned in the context of Western civilizations and cultures. There are these two imperatives at work: first, not to get lost as an individual in the rigorous attempt to establish a continuum in the biography of the collective. This is what I mean in saying that the poet must be at the same time solitary and solidary, following the formula of Albert Camus, which I had forgotten, then rediscovered. Solitary: there is preservation of the individual as a resource. Solidary: there is searching for the collective continuum in time, as a poetics. So I would say that in a second instance, for a poet, a politics of his own individuality's maintenance is sketched out simultaneously with a poetics of searching for his community. You will notice that I invert the function of these terms, 'politics' and 'poetics', and not according to their common acceptations, but as delineating a new dialectics. Just as in the relation between the 'vidas' and 'razos' of the troubadours, the poem occurs in the act of living, and the change occurs in the exchange.

Considering, searching for continuum in the collective biography, or in other words, forging, constructing, approaching or sketching out a new conception of history, seems to me just as important a matter as the first aspect (maintenance of the individual) that I have developed. This is because Western writing has contributed to the emergence of a notion of History that must, I contend, be brought into question. For the time being, I would resume this point by alluding to a formula which is perhaps obscure, but which establishes a sort of continuity not only within the reconstructed biographies of collectivities, but also within their rediscovered relations with the biographies of other communities: 'There where the histories of peoples finally join together, is where History with a capital H ends'.

As I see it, this primary fragmentation of dates, this discontinuity of the collective and communal biography, corresponds to the punctual expression of the diversity of landscapes. Just as collective memory has been scratched out, so have landscapes been ravaged. Learning in one's own life how to read the landscape or how to dwell within it is, to my mind, learning how to reconstitute its continuation or its proceeding: it is giving oneself the means of recomposing that other continuum, of the collective biography. Today, the reading of landscapes, just as much as archaeology or numismatics, helps in understanding the episodes and circumstances of the transformation of peoples and their communities. For example, this technique has been abundantly employed in recent times in the study of the formation of France. Reading landscapes is ultimately a way of accounting for time. In the same vein, decoding (which is the opposite of clearing away) and frequenting countries in their fragmentation permits us, through poetic reconstitution, to verify how landscapes have never been consenting settings, but instead, active and constitutive elements of the diverse poetics put into play or into expression by individuals or communities. An example of this is how impressive the reading of the Martinican landscape has been for me. In observing what has happened, one notices that during the time of slavery all of the black people's cabins were in the lowlands, and the houses of the planters, the colonists, were built upon the crests, the heights. It is the classic schema of Habitation, of the unity of production,

'The subtlety, or innocent and instinctive artfulness, of the poet'   19

from the seventeenth century onward: the master's house dominates the cabins of the slaves or the workers. But gradually as a small middle class is formed among the Martinicans, this class somehow moves up along the crests, so that the landscape changes for and within the sensibilities of the Martinicans themselves. For living in the depths, surviving in the ravines where one is weakened and vulnerable to the torrents of mud stirred up by cyclones, to the violent collapses resulting from earthquakes, etc., is not at all informed by the same sense of livelihood as climbing or ascending the landscape, where one is deafened by the wind.

Precisely at this moment, and I mean the moment where topographical divisions were decided, the natural movement of those who were called runaway slaves or maroons is to *climb* into the forest. In reality, this movement is cultural. I have always been struck by the fact that when Fidel Castro wanted to return to Cuba with his future *barbudos*,* when he could have hidden or lost himself in Havana among more than a million inhabitants, he solemnly announced instead that he was going to climb into the Sierra Maestra, where only a preserved nature could protect him. This was a form of marooning, culturally a decision to live in the landscape in the manner of the old runaway slaves. This link to the landscape makes a link to history.

What I am repeating here permits us to enter into the uncertainty of individual biography, of the poet's biography, in that through absences it is quite a different matter. It seems to me that secondary elements of this biography are decided by a number of more determining moments, and that these other more determining moments are linked to the three aspects that I have just evoked in a global way: 1) biographies of the collectivity, or at least, their reconstruction, and 2) 'universal' History, as opposed to the peoples' histories, and 3) speech restored to the setting.

A.L. There are several issues in what you have said, and I would like to specify them quickly in relation to your personal position. The question here would be the poet's place in History and in the collectivity. It seems to me that there are two reference points in your discourse: a recognition of the very large and important determinations, but also the other side of the problem, which would be to show at what moment the poet himself becomes a determinant. If poetry is something, if literature is something,

---

* *Barbudos* are bearded revolutionaries. The term was first used to describe the rebels involved in the Cuban Revolution (1953–59).

if your activity as a writer is something, they cannot be limited to the reflection of historical conditions.

What this means is that they cannot be completely understood from what you have called determinations. In this sense, whenever you write, whenever you publish, whenever you are read, you are intervening in history. You are shaping a part of history. And you are intervening in the collectivity, or at least in its movement and its present. How do you conceive of this intervention? To what degree do you believe that literature is that which escapes determinants in order to create other determinations?

É.G. One could respond in an overall way, in a conceptual manner. But I also believe in the subtlety or instinctive artfulness of the poet, a subtlety and artfulness that the practice of the poem allows him. Of course, a poet does inscribe general propositions in his project, such as those I have just described. But it is equally evident that a poet does not obey or conform to general ideas that he has formulated, even those that he has formulated *for himself*. General ideas, the project, are there to set up the track, as one would mark off a trail in the forest. But we don't know where this track will lead. The plants indicating a spring are hidden, the trails leading nowhere all too obvious. We have no determinants, no line of sight indicating a goal. Moreover, history, as I believe it is conceived, comprises no aim. It is not a process which takes off from one place, has a motor at its disposal and proceeds toward another place. So that is the first approach. I'll repeat, it is the subtlety or instinctive artfulness of the poet which would ultimately keep him from consenting or sacrificing to determinations that he himself would have considered very obvious. The second response that I might formulate is that ultimately, the revolution of poetry, which is to dig underneath the real and to try to point out what is not at all given in appearance, leads us far, not far, in fact, from the troubadours.

This very activity can, all while following the determinations that I have mentioned, incline us to take those determinations the wrong way. For example, poetry and engaging with poetry led me to consider relationships to land. And I noted that a relationship to land, which one can live without ever worrying too much about it, is a relation of property in Western writing, even if it is also a profound relation, even if it is also an organic relation. This question could have affected the child that I had been, who had in part grown up on Habitations, or Plantations of agricultural exploitation, sites of absolute expropriation. I'll remark that in the texts of pre-Columbian Indians, they never considered themselves as proprietors, but rather as guardians of the land. And there we have an eminently poetic proposition, because it changes the way we see the landscape. This is reinforced by the fact that during my life I have very often consented to what I would call wandering, which is not the same as blindly roaming, but which is going elsewhere, perhaps to escape the temptation of property. Another kind of relation to the landscape in which one exists, or in which one has been placed, or in which one has been born, is thus introduced, different in that the landscape is not considered as one's proper and legitimate territory.

Thus, the thought of wandering, of seeing elsewhere, of 'displacing', a thought that refuses the perspective of conquest and expansion as they have been so sumptuously and mortally practiced by occidental cultures, this thought changes the relation to the landscape. My own modes of 'learning' the Martinican landscape have been just as much about distancing myself from it as about scattering myself within it. I have seen from afar the fables about the hilltops, the sufferings of the cultivated plains, the hope of the shorelines. I had seen from close up the misery of the heights, the craftiness and obstinacy of the flatlands, the illusion of the beaches and seaside cliffs. The dialectic of these two courses has followed the slope of the Lézarde River. Once discovered, the divisions of the landscape converge in its unity. And there we have a poetic proposition: as a counter-current to the determining will to find a continuum in the landscape or in the collective biography, this thought of wandering introduces new relations to the country, a poetic opposition to the injunctions of system that would govern the frequentation of the country and thus impose an altered view of the biographical continuum of its community.

The thought of system is the thought of territory. The thought of wandering is the thought of non-system and of the land. The thought of the landscape is not a groundwork, but rather, a relation. This seems important to me and responds to the question of how one can keep from being predetermined by the very determinations that one has conceived or proposed. And also the question of how one can keep from succumbing to mechanisms of being and seeming. Wandering is not exploration, whether colonial or not. Neither knowledge nor thought of gain enters into its movement. All of this work is possible only through a sort of instinctive artfulness (it is necessary that I repeat it here). The relation to the land, and to the landscape, which is the land clothed in its own continuum, goes through the outspread and multiplied root, which does not eviscerate the land. (However, there is also at times a nobility of property, just as much as obstinacy, and a sordid plundering.)

A.L. The poet proposes, reveals to himself determinations which are a trace without announced teleology. In this formula I see an act of liberty in the sense that you separate yourself from determinations as they are deductively imposed, positing that there is to begin with the choice of liberating oneself in relation to them. They then leave the domain of absolute determination to become something that is a part of the poetic play or artfulness.

É.G. To appreciate the movement that we have tackled in such a general and conceptual way, I'll advance several observations. First, for an Antillean, especially at the time when I was a young man, going toward somewhere else was at the same time a calling and a necessity: one needs to leave a place if one really wants to hold onto it. (Absolute misery is what makes you leave your place only in hopelessness, in search of the merest breath of air.) My personal history has always begun with a departure. Leaving the heights of the Bezaudin Hill (in Sainte Marie) for the cane crops of the Lamentin plain is one of my childhood myths, as I was scarcely a month old and was carried in my mother's arms. And then, a departure for France at eighteen years of age with the meagre advantages of a scholarship student. It is in the same way that the history of black collectivities in the Americas begins with an uprooting from elsewhere (from Africa) to arrive at a 'here' which is for me as for so many others, familiar Antillean lands, and all around, the infinity of the Americas, with its undiminished horizon.

Individual history today runs in a counter-current to the old collective history: one is no longer the victim of an uprooting from an elsewhere (from Africa), one leaves instead from the here and now to go to another elsewhere, to Europe, for example. It's a sort of return, but roundabout. It is what I have called in chapters of *Caribbean Discourse* an avatar of the necessity of detour in Antillean thought. For the detour introduces an intelligence of the obstacle, a faculty for working one's way around, the advantage of the dodge, the art of the relative, and so many other recourses. Individual history, or biography, is not linked to the situation. One can leave without asking any questions. But leaving while asking whether or not one will clarify the problem of the relation to the land (poetically, I am not speaking here of politics or economics), then it is necessary to begin with an uprooting. Biography is first of all linked to an almost organic drive. And these are the wanderings of the student who leaves to study in Paris, at the Sorbonne (a word that rings in the ear), who enters into contact with French intellectuals, poets, and writers of his generation. The nearly empty streets were great discussion halls. It would be interesting for me to examine a bit the nature of the intellectual or poetic relationships that I maintained with young poets or young writers, with which ones, and why. But they were friends, and we shared no theory.

The other dimension is the quality of the relations that I established, on the one hand, with this centre constituted by France, Paris, and more generally, by the West, and on the other, with people one could really only know in this elsewhere, in the capitals of these elsewheres.

That is where the repercussion of anti-colonialist struggles took place, struggles in which I was somewhat involved. So there are these aspects: affinities with French poets, writers, and intellectuals; and then, solidarity with colonial struggles; and the very thought of decolonization. These relations are in some way not determined, but oriented or coloured by the very act of poetry, the very practice of poetic exercise.

This is also where there might be an equivalence to set up with the passion of the troubadours. Wasn't their lure to poetry also coloured by their wanderings? By that I mean the relationship they were able to inaugurate or maintain with other intellectuals, such as the university scholars of the time. Did they have such relationships, and if not, why? Or with other communities, such as Arab cultures? And with other spiritualities? The Jewish Cabala? Did the troubadours' writing have a link to the speech of the Cathars? There are theories upholding this view. In other words, does not the obstinacy of poetic writing colour the vision that one creates of the world, the wanderings one takes up within it, the relationships one establishes, while at the same time marking or directing the biographies which one ascribes to oneself?

A.L. The Antillean who goes to Paris – elsewhere –, does he ascend or does he descend? I would really like to understand. He ascends to Paris, no?

É.G. Do you mean does he aspire to something superior? No, 'he does not aspire to ascend', if that is what you mean. The displacement is transversal, often lived as a painful emigration. Elsewhere, elsewhere. Not above or below, but Elsewhere. Along with that, there is often an unconscious drive, which recognizes no real interpretable motivation. Immigrations are most often merciless, and always fractal. Your remark still presents the great interest in marking off a sort of poetics of displacement, which is manifestly there.

Ascending or descending, which is never transcendence, only has meaning in a primordial space. This is because there (here), the heights have a significance for you, as do the lowlands.

'I am going up into town, I am going down to Caffard Cove': you know where your point of suspension is. You're either running into hiding or not.

Or: 'I'm going down into town', if you're in another place in the country, from where the wind blows.

But: 'I'm going to France', or 'I'm leaving for France', – and that's enough to stir the old melancholy, like the hoarse call of the great ships.

For the heights and the depths are measured by the wind, but when we are talking about the sea, the prairies and the vast steppes, the flat expanse has only infinity as its rule.

A.L. An interesting problem for me in consideration of the troubadours is what they have called *fin'amour*, or courtly love. Very often, these poets are Western poets in that they are feudal lords who in a very concrete sense have a proprietary relationship to the land. The question of woman's status is already posed at this level, in that during this time a woman is nothing but an exchange value for a territorial possession. She is exchanged, given, appropriated through marriage, etc. It is striking that the troubadour lady has essentially no relationship whatsoever with the socio-political reality of the time.

In the reality of the feudal relation and the relation of absolute vassalage that a woman has with respect to a man at that time, there is probably a deficiency addressed by poetry: through the invention of *fin'amor*, the lady effectively becomes the feudal lord who always says 'no', who makes herself off-limits to the poet, and who symbolically takes his place. The intent is that the poet always be desiring, and thus, always writing, as the poems are also missives to the Lady. These missives are sent in the hope that she will give in to the poet's desire. And of course, she always refuses this desire.

É.G. Mystical thought also edifies a kind of readjustment to woman's status, to her traditionally unbearable condition. Mystical thought affirmed that woman is infinitely inferior to man in strength (and perhaps also in mind), but infinitely superior to man in grace. This is what you have sketched out with regard to the troubadours, the fact that woman is placed in a position of non-territorialization, and this is what one might call her superiority in grace. But she is never a serf, rarely middle-class, and almost always a great noblewoman. She is not a woman, but the wife or the daughter of a nobleman. As you say, the troubadours are often great feudal lords. Perhaps this is an instance of alienation within alienation.

Let me return to the *fin'amor* of these troubadours. How could we, as Antilleans, associate ourselves with such an ideal, emerging as we do from the hell of slavery and Plantations, in which woman is less than a slave, or even, the slave of masters and slaves? She has no means of refusal. Could what you call courtliness have currency in a penal colony? Today, arising from the hard and actual struggles of dominated peoples, we collectively have the possibility of trying to overcome oppression or colonization by bringing about another vision of the world, which for me is a vision of the poetics of Relation. In this, we are inventing different forms of networks, another relationship to the Other. And perhaps other impulses of love? This poetics of Relation could be applied to the humanities, just as the poetics of *fin'amor* could have been applied to the situation of all women – through a utopia that would have veiled an inconceivable condition. Is this another alienation within another alienation?

When I arrived in Paris, I had two kinds of associations which, schizophrenically, were not joined and did not overlap. On the one hand, there were naturally occurring relationships made out of complicity with my Antillean friends and comrades– Martinicans, Guadeloupeans, or Guyanese. On the other hand, there was my association with young poets and French writers such as Roger Giroux, Jean Laude, Henri Pichette, Maurice Roche, Jean Paris, Paul Meyer and Jacques Charpier. It was also in Paris that I met Kateb Yacine and Tchicaya U'Tamsi: all of the writers outside the center met up with each other in the Center. It seems to me that I met the French poets mentioned here out of a sort of necessity that we will call poetic. A vital energy matched me up with the poets of the South. I remember that at the time my Antillean friends, who were all childhood acquaintances, were kind enough to accept it, but really didn't understand why I so assiduously kept up with all these French people, because there was perhaps no reason to associate with them. This was not at all through antiracist racism, nor through rejection: it was simply that they didn't quite get it. Perhaps it was also that they didn't understand what it was for me to want to be a writer or poet. There were so many other pressing matters.

I remember that, later on, when I found myself engaged in political activities, Antillean comrades who participated in the same movements asked in my regard, and with a wondering solicitude:

'But what does he do?'

– He's a writer, a poet.
– Yes, but aside from that? What does he do?
– He's a writer', replied Albert Béville,* kindly smiling. (In literature this is Paul Niger, who was one of my closest friends.)

'Yes, but aside from that, what does he do?'

A necessary utilitarianism for those who are striving to survive, and who don't have the time.

In me there was the appearance of a schism: on the one hand, an experiential solidarity with my Antillean friends, and on the other, an essential solitude, the individuation of the poetic act which I nevertheless shared with the French poets, without our ever having to formulate it.

Associating with them, I thus entered into the Parisian, French, literary milieu, not with worldly objectives, but to participate in work that was then being done in the literary sphere in a very active, concrete, real and profound way, such as in the work of the *Lettres Nouvelles*** about Maurice Nadeau and Maurice Saillet. Maurice Roche, Henri Pichette, and Roger Giroux are all marginal,*** but not at all in the sense of being antisocial or hippies. They are instead marginal in that, while being extremely diverse poets and writers, they all conceive that poetry lays the foundation for its own dimension and quest, its own necessity – indeed, an absolute poematic necessity.

I experienced a true joy in meeting these writers, whatever their future might have been, or mine. For example, I think that Giroux is a great writer and poet of contemporary French literature, but he is unknown. Maurice Roche is a very great writer, but his work is not received as it should be. None of these poets is preoccupied with his own station. They are not men of the market or of fashion.

This sort of schizophrenia in me really didn't exist. There wasn't an opposition between my Antillean and French associations. We were, both Antilleans and Frenchmen of that generation, in search of a new poetics, or

---

* Albert Béville (1915–62) – better known under his pen name Paul Niger – was a poet and political activist from Guadeloupe. With Glissant, he founded the Front Antillo-Guyanais in 1959 to campaign for independence for the French overseas departments. Béville died in the crash of an Air France flight in Guadeloupe in June 1962.
** *Les Lettres Nouvelles* was a literary periodical founded in 1953 by Maurice Nadeau and Maurice Saillet. Glissant was among its early contributors.
*** Maurice Roche (1924–97) was a composer, writer, artist and journalist; Henri Pichette (1924–2000) was a writer, dramatist and poet; Roger Giroux (1925–74) was a poet and translator. All three were contributors to *Les Lettres Nouvelles*.

of a new sense of presence in the world. I remember one of Henri Pichette's texts: 'Literature is beautiful only in the bed of the world'. In this regard, there was no rupture with my belonging to an Antillean universe. The vain schism didn't take hold, it was only an appearance. It seems to me that in those meetings and at that time it even coalesced into a means of poetic logic, which continued in one direction and in another: here-there.

♦ 3 ♦

'The aim of writing is not to incite political action'

Édouard Glissant. I remember designating the notion of centre, of periphery, in *The Ripening*,* where, to speak about Paris, France, and the government, I use the word 'Centre' with a capital C.

That was the first time I used the word. The problem is that I was in fact writing *The Ripening* when I was already in France, which is to say, already in the Centre. One can truly understand the relationship of a centre to a periphery only by having an experience of the Centre. This is because the centre designates itself as centre, but conveys what it is only by being unmarked as the Centre. Seen from the periphery, representation of the centre can appear to be mythical.

Writing *in* the Centre, one becomes aware that there is perhaps an ex-centric thinking, displaced outside the norm of the centre. Without going into bombast and excesses, I can say that when I was writing *The Ripening* I began to understand that there is a fundamental idea of ex-centric thought, interesting in relation to a form of centred thought. That's the experience that I had in France, in Paris, an experience that I have related in a book, *The Sun of Consciousness*.** In it, I go back to the themes of a poetics of measure and immoderation, and the comparison of landscapes between themselves: the landscape of the spring and the meadow so dear to the Middle Ages studied by Ernst Robert Curtius,*** and the landscape of the

---

* *The Ripening* – French title: *La Lézarde* – was Glissant's first novel, published in 1958. It won the prestigious Prix Renaudot.
** *The Sun of Consciousness* – French title: *Soleil de la Conscience* – was Glissant's first book, published in 1956. This book-length essay introduced many of the key concepts in Glissant's work. It inaugurated the *Poétique* (Poetics) strand of his work.
*** Ernst Robert Curtius (1886–1956) was a German literary scholar and medievalist. His best-known study is *European Literature and the Latin Middle Ages*, first published in German in 1948.

earthquake and the jungle, the jungle landscape that I was beginning then to detect and appreciate in the poetics of Saint-John Perse.* As a result, the fact of having gone to, lived in, and experienced the Centre, not only as a mythical centre but as what it truly was, undoubtedly authorized me to set up this separation between an ex-centric way of thinking and a centred thought, a separation that I later tried to establish as often as possible. Moreover, the French poets whom I had befriended were themselves outliers in relation to the centred discourses which surrounded them, but which held little interest for them. These were ex-centric personalities, not in their lives, but in their poetry making, their writing, and their poetics. The phenomenon always impassioned me. Giroux, for example, was already tending toward a kind of silence, a sort of paring down of speech into absolute silence. If I couldn't share this with him, I could still appreciate it. And then there were the poets, such as Jacques Charpier and Jean Laude,** who displayed a rare sort of confidence in rhetorical speech and gesture. This position interested me still more, since I thought (and continue to think) that the rhetoric of our writing, of us other poetic writers who were, shall we say, generally from the South, passes through this confidence in our language. We are not fearful in this regard, we are not stingy with respect to words, we are neither prudent nor reticent, and we have no shame of accumulation, repetition, or baroque scale. These two rhetorical orders – the word that runs dry and the word which multiplies—I cannot say that we designated them in a decisive manner at the time, but we were conscious of them, we had a premonition of them, and we predicted them. My association with these poets, who were all among my very best friends, was for me something remarkable.

I've already spoken about the debate that existed in my life between this frequentation and my organic relationship with my Antillean brothers. For example, when I participated in the Antillo-Guyanese Front, in Paris (in 1960), well, my French friends knew nothing of this aspect of my existence, just as the Antilleans knew nothing about what I discussed with these same poets. In other words, there was a sort of established division. But as I've already affirmed, and I want to reiterate the point, this division really didn't exist: what I was looking for in both cases was that ex-centric

---

* Saint-John Perse was the pseudonym of Alexis Léger (1887–1975). He was a French poet and diplomat, awarded the Nobel Prize in Literature in 1960. Glissant had a particular interest in Perse as he was born in Guadeloupe.
** Charpier and Laude were poets who belonged to the Parisian literary circles Glissant frequented in the 1950s.

discourse, and in both cases I found resources and useful assistance for this very quest. I repeat it because repetition and resifting help me delve into the problem.

In a completely innocent and instinctive manner, and not at all in a learned way, I want to emphasize this concerning the struggles of decolonization: for a time, they constituted the veritable decentralization of thought, practiced, among others, by Franz Fanon. But I was perturbed by the way that these struggles had been continued, for example, in Africa or in a number of other countries in the world that I knew, with so many deaths, so many sacrifices: I had the presentiment that these struggles had been conducted according to the same model of those who were being opposed. And it was later, at a tranquil distance, that I tried to see how this model had determined the struggles. I arrived at the question of identity, of the definition of identity as Being. These struggles of decolonization, which had necessitated so many sacrifices, so many deaths, and so many wars, had been pursued on the very principle that the West had formulated, the principle of identity as a unique root. I didn't hesitate to join in these struggles, but I was beset by misgivings. The decolonizations had been followed by a series of agonizing disappointments: peoples who had heroically fought were afterwards torn apart in a fierce, internal way. Without doing any critical work, they adopted ideas of territorial power, of military force, the very concept of the State, and the rest, all of which opened them to corruption. This demonstrated by contrast that the decolonizations had been absolutely necessary, but that, even if they were not any less heroic, they had not been accompanied by an adequate work of critical reflection with respect to the very ideas that the West had proposed to the world. There was much more to this than the expression of an intellectual viewpoint. It was a troubling misgiving that was to colour my reflections, and more importantly, the reflections of many others.

Alexandre Leupin. I am sure that calling into question, not the colonial struggles themselves, but the manner in which they were carried out, had consequences for you concerning your conception of writing.

É.G. Yes, and in a direct way, because the question that I was always asked at that time (and which, by the way, no one ever asks me now) was multiple, and formulated in this manner: 'But finally, tell us, for whom do you write? Could what you write be understood by a person who cuts sugar cane, or by a Tonkinese farmer/farmhand? Isn't the first function of writing to contribute to the heroic struggles being waged?' Generally speaking, it was not a question of political writing in the ordinary sense that one attributes to it in the West, but instead, the question of writing intervening in the quick of combat as a means of hastening this combat and influencing its outcome. I was always very categorical in my response. Writing did not have the function of inciting political action (a great theme during the era when the Sartrian conception of writing prevailed). This vision seemed false to me. Perhaps I wasn't analysing it in all its subtleties and details. Still, I thought that if one devoted writing solely to the aims of a popular struggle, a community or national struggle, and if in the work of writing one forgot what there was behind these struggles, meaning the most unobtrusive foundations of a culture, its opacities of Being and tremblings of knowledge, then the work of the writer was not being accomplished, but instead, and no less necessary, the work of a pamphleteer or an engaged journalist or militant eager to get results.

Getting to what there was behind this struggle, to whatever there was of a cultural awareness behind the struggle, often meant being brought back to the perspective of the one who says: 'Yes, but you only have to describe the life of the people, their condition, etc., and culture will be transmitted in that way'. I wasn't at all sure that this was the case, and I am still unconvinced. At that time, I considered most of the engaged, militant, and suffering descriptions of struggling colonized countries to be just as vain and folkloric as the paradisiacal descriptions produced by colonization: in neither case were the underlying terms elucidated. If one wanted to sketch out or approximate orders, disorders, points, lines of projection and prospect, it was necessary to go further and deeper than this primary militancy of writing. I am sure (without actually saying it to myself or others) that I was at some time restricted by this displacement of writing. This is perhaps why my life as a militant was unknown to my French poet friends and that my participation in poetic exposés in France was not followed by my militant friends. This fact created a certain discomfort in me. What I believe, and I'll say it again, is first of all that my position – not consenting simply and ingenuously to the primacy (primal nature) of the struggle – was the right one, and it was difficult to resist this imperative at the time. In the second place (and I'm not saying that this proved me right, because it's absurd to think about being right or wrong under any circumstances whatsoever), the course of events clearly showed the inadequacy of our work on these issues, an inadequacy that remains to this very moment as we speak. To put it plainly, in the panorama of our current world, the proliferation of writings has not yet sketched out the structuring vectors of what lies underneath (but not *in depth*), of what we don't yet see. Again, the reality of writing is to try to reveal these structuring vectors, which concern relations between cultures just as much as the definition of the cultures themselves. If we didn't do one together with the other, it seems to me we would be missing the mark. A great many writers of the countries of the South have undergone these upheavals. You see how the *continuum of the collective*, so difficult to restore, ultimately corresponds to the *discontinuity of the person*, which must be withstood no matter what.

A.L. Is it necessary for an Antillean, North American, Columbian, etc., to write for Antilleans, North Americans, Colombians on Antillean, etc. subjects? It's a very simple question, but I think that you surprise your public a lot because you refuse to be relegated to one category or another.

É.G. I'm in agreement with you on this issue, but we have to be careful: it is not a simple dichotomy. The question is not at all whether an Antillean or North American writer should write for 'his/her' public on issues that interest a much wider audience. What about a Dane or a Montenegrin? Let's posit that writing should go beyond those phenomena, even if one is writing about subjects that concern one's own land, one's own entourage, and the problems that afflict them. For example, Faulkner wrote only about his own Mississippi, or only about the problems of the deep South in the United States. Very rare are the Faulknerian texts that 'take place' in London or in Europe during the First World War. But it is in the processes of writing that he absolutely goes beyond this localization, it is the process of writing that permits him at the same time to veil and unveil his subject. And we know that the nature of his subject leads him not to recite directly this unnameable subject (the damnation of the southern United States), but to invent almost in spite of himself the very form of modern literatures, *differed writing*, which will consist of speaking without speaking while speaking. It is the process of writing which adds this something, and which makes it so that what Faulkner writes is valuable for everyone in the world.

What I call exotic or folkloric literature is a literature which, in its writing, concerns only its own object, the object of the work. It is in the successions of writing that transcendence occurs. It is altogether illuminating that, as regards Faulkner, it is the writing that discomfited, shocked, and bogged readers down in their approach to his work. If Faulkner had explored the same themes in an availably folkloric style, specifically as a *story-teller* (which would have resulted in something far removed from his narrative detours), he surely would have been more appreciated, but would have been classified as a secondary writer. Certainly, one can unfold stories of and about one's own land, but it can be done only with a complete absence of complacency in writing. Another example: Aimé Césaire displays a merciless lucidity in his *writing of the Martinican land*, and that is the asceticism of *Notebook of a Return to My Native Land*.* Writing, through its own process, seeks something beyond narration alone, and in so doing, necessarily transcends the framework which it describes, which it writes. In the actual world, that something else which it seeks is, I'll repeat, whatever is unprecedented, unwarranted, invisible and unheard in the texture of relations between humanities and cultures. That which sets up and constitutes the reality of what I call the actual Chaos world of society. All nuances, individual and collective, and all riches, of structures and twists, undergo this process. Centres and peripheries are reciprocal within it. The writer changes perspective.

The question would thus be: is there a limit to writing, even as its object could seem limited on the horizon of the world? My response, a truly personal one, proposes that the only limit of writing would be for it to renounce saying everything, or to pretend to say only nothing. Between these distances, Relation wanders and enlightens.

---

* *Notebook of a Return to the Native Land* – French title: *Cahier d'un retour au pays natal* – is a poem by Martinican writer and statesman Aimé Césaire published initially in 1939.

4

'A variegated pattern of transformations …: on the epic'

Alexandre Leupin. I'll start off here with a remark in the *Poetics of Relation*, which I will paraphrase: 'For a nation-state to exist, it must speak itself'. This sudden remark enlightens me on the function of that grand epic text of French tradition, *The Song of Roland*.* In the language of this foundational work, the names 'France' and 'French' are promoted in writing for the first time. They undoubtedly existed in orality, but take on a whole other dimension by virtue of being changed to the status of a written text. What *The Song of Roland* reveals is that this promotion departs from a series of negotiations, ruptures, and massacres that ultimately deliver, not an emperor in the Roman style, but a king, a monarch linked to a nation that speaks one sole language. What *The Song of Roland* shows us is that this process is absolutely blood-stained. It relies on what René Girard has called the scapegoat.** We can fairly easily show that Roland, and all the Saracens (who should be considered fantasy Saracens, as they have no relation to the Muslims of the time), and Ganelon, ultimately appear as though they are all designated feudal lords. Charlemagne provokes their death, kills them, executes them, to effectuate the transformation from a fairly vague concept of empire to the notion of a nation-state – a notion based upon a foundational violence. In my opinion, this process, as it is described so notably in *The Song of Roland* (because it amplifies an entire history), marks all of the

---

* *The Song of Roland* is an epic poem that recounts the Battle of Roncevaux of 778, during the reign of Charlemagne. It is considered by many to be the oldest surviving work of French literature and was composed in the period between 1040 and 1115.

** René Girard (1923–2015) was a French literary critic and philosopher who spent much of his literary career in the USA. Among his best known books is *The Scapegoat*, first published in French as *Le Bouc émissaire* in 1982.

groundwork of the nation-state in Europe. With extraordinary clarity, *The Song* shows us that this very process is infinitely gory.

Édouard Glissant. I believe that the idea of a king mystically linked to a nation, which is not yet a nation but already a country, appears during the Merovingian period ('the fabulous race', according to Gérard de Sède).* As an epic poem, *The Song of Roland* represents the consecration of imperialist activity (in the sense of a conquering empire) by the Carolingians, at least, *up until* Charlemagne. The empire is multilingual; the people do not speak the same language at Aix-la-Chapelle and in the South. This return to the empire is a return to Roman repression; in these particular circumstances, Roman repression is represented by the Holy Roman Empire, soon to become Germanic. It will be a long time before the kings of France abdicate the illusory pretention of acceding to the imperial throne, of taking over the succession of Charlemagne, emperor of the West. This vision perhaps upholds the legitimacy of those upstarts who became palace administrators, the first Capetians (who stopped the Arab invasion, instigated the First Crusade, and then the fall of Jerusalem – which are all rather imperialist actions), and maybe even that other upstart, Napoleon Bonaparte, who re-enacted the imperial dream. To align our viewpoints, let's say that *The Song of Roland* is the moment when an emerging monolingual nation seeks to buttress itself by a reference to the multilingual (Roman) empire, which is no longer anything more than an absent ideal, if not a lure.

Here I'd like to make an essential point: one of the principles of the epic, borne out in *The Song of Roland*, is dealing with or proceeding from the standpoint, not so much of a victim (the notion of the scapegoat in the way that René Girard develops it), but of a real defeat. If the Saracens in *The Song of Roland* are operetta figures, the defeat at Roncesvalles is established fact: it is an historical defeat.

A.L. Christian Basques from the mountains crushed the rear guard of the Carolingian army .... Very little relation to the grandiose fresco depicted by *The Song of Roland* ....

---

* Gérard de Sède (1921–2004) was a French author associated with various surrealist organisations. He belonged to the literary circles Glissant frequented in the 1950s. De Sède wrote several books on the Merovingian dynasty, notable amongst which is *L'Or de Rennes* (1967).

É.G. But a defeat in any case, and it had to be specifically captured by epic transfiguration. I have things to say here about the epic genre. I think that the sacrificial concept in epic needs to be nuanced. It is partially verified, especially when the epic becomes tragic. Still, to my mind, the most important point is that all epic is articulated around a defeat, or at most, an ambiguous victory. An ambiguous victory of the Greeks against the Trojans, an ambiguous victory of Ulysses after his odyssey. Epic smacks of bitterness, and therein lies its incredible compass: it is lucid, but tries to sidetrack us. It's as if epic speech were begging the question: yes, we did this, but to what effect? In any event, epic proceeds from a defeat. For example, what is astounding if we look closely at the contemporary history of the North American continent, the United States has made epics out of its defeats, and not from its victories. Consider the Alamo (and not the conquest of Texas), the Civil War (for people of the South), the defeat of General Custer at Little Big Horn, Pearl Harbor (and not the final overthrow of Japan), or the Vietnam War. The United States has created cinematic epics with its defeats, but not so much with its victories in the two great World Wars, which may still come after a latency period. And the furbelows of *Gone with the Wind* notwithstanding, it is still the great defeat of the South that fuelled the epic work of Faulkner.

But let's return to the question of language. Several elements seem essential to me. First of all, the element of time, the temporal span. The example of *The Song of Roland* is quite apt here. If it is a constitutive moment, it is because it publicizes a process that extends from Late Antiquity and which is very slowly and progressively accentuated: the activity of France as an entity. In a like manner, languages aggregate themselves very slowly as they are being constituted, and they do so indifferently. Scholars are perhaps aware of these transformations, of the appearances of languages. However, at present they can still only record the necessity of language in any new economic or political structures which are adopted. What I would like is for us to be able to truly expose how, for example, the procedures of linguistic creolization became operative in the different regions of what would eventually become France. And to see how this phenomenon was tied up with basic economic organizations of the time such as the farm (*villa*) and the first cities in a contemporary sense (not fortresses), organizations which were beginning to appear and which support linguistic process. I think it evident that, at this time, Being could be defined by language. As language develops, Being evolves as well, as witnessed by that illustrious seventeenth-century grammarian who sighed upon his deathbed: 'I go, or I am going, to die, one and the other is said, or are said', and then expired from organic failure and syntactic disturbance (vainglory?).

In a common sense, and not in a Sophistic interpretation, we have gradually assumed the habit of saying that language is Being. It is also noteworthy that this process confirmed or emphasized *the very idea* that there is such a thing as Being. In what was to follow in the West, Catholicism or Christianity would elaborate the underlying dogma that the entire factual element, the *apparatus* of History aims to unveil Being in increasingly historical, or recognizable, forms. This process will culminate in Hegelian thought, according to which History is an avatar of Reason. In the Western world, when it was said, 'Tell me what language you speak, and I will tell you who you are', what was meant in a learned sense was: 'Tell me which language you speak, and I will tell you how you participate in Being'.

An important element developed, not with invasions, but with colonizations. There is a difference between invasions and colonizations. Paradoxically, stronger images of colonization have remained with us: the slice of meat underneath the saddle, miraculous conversions, and so many other episodes, but we still don't know what Captain Marchand yelled out when his skirmishers burned the library of Timbuktu.*

You will have noticed that, in their very character, invasions belong to the Middle Ages, whereas colonizations are a feature of the Renaissance. Invasions are not about discovering the world. The difference is not only chronological, since it is ideology that creates and hallows colonization: the Renaissance always strives to legitimate expansion, contrary to what all-powerful nations will do later in the nineteenth century, at the height of their influence over the world. Invasions knew no crises of conscience.

The first difference is that, with invasions, entire peoples are displaced and conquer others; they gradually change, are changed and transformed by their conquests. In colonization, peoples are not displaced. Only colonists, as many individuals as are delegated by colonization, are displaced. But something is displaced, and that something is language. Languages of colonization are languages that have been displaced. Because of this fact, those languages have informed and interested (in the fullest sense of the term) other people who, without having moved themselves, find themselves prey to a new language. The language has been displaced, but the historical avatar of Being as Being has not.

---

* Jean-Baptiste Marchand (1863–1934) was a French military officer and explorer in Africa. He is remembered for commanding the French expeditionary force during the Fashoda Incident of 1898.

In colonization, the mass of a population is not displaced. The French did not move wholesale into Africa, nor did the British leave as an entire body for the Americas, with the exception of the ex-centric, reclusive, or banished, and the delegates for colonization. Populating colonies never empty out parent states. It's not an invasion, but a colonization, which will define a new direction of language. Here we find a language that has been displaced without an accompanying displacement of its support, a language that is moved and undergoing transformation elsewhere, without a displacement of the majority of people who speak it. There are provincial administrators of the language, the colonists, who are at times linguistically feeble; such is the case of the first French colonists in the Antilles, who speak the illiterate, slangy, and very salty jargon of Norman and Breton sailors. Yet it is neither the historical support of language nor its linguistic vector that are displaced. The language largely dominates in the place where it has been transplanted, but it is still subject to dramatic weaknesses, even risks of extinction, which authorities must thwart at every turn. As for autochthonous languages, they aren't even mentioned.

A.L. Language is displaced from the perspective of the master, toward the slave, and the master is immobile. For Hegel, the slave is the active subject of history.

É.G. Yes, but if Hegel has very carefully considered the structure of this process, he hasn't examined its content or substance very thoroughly. The interesting point here is that language, if we may say it, provokes schizophrenias and becomes itself schizophrenic: it divides within itself. And, from that time on, it stops existing in a continuum, a historical progressivity slow enough to permit those transformations which are not at first sight perceived. Language enters into an historical precipitation, a sudden process of discontinuity in relation to the support, the historical avatar constituted by the people who initially spoke it. It is superimposed upon other people and other languages, it is submitted to different figures and circuits, and it returns by ricochet to its very source.

This phenomenon assumes extremely diverse forms. The language can become an official language alongside the indigenous mother tongues, which are then dominated (I refer here to the case of French or English in Africa). And it can change in nature through being practiced by populations finding themselves in contact with new realities and having an acute consciousness of what a language is, as in the United States; this was not necessarily the case of the medieval epochs which we have discussed. And language can constitute within its own self another language. This is what occurred in Quebec and in Creole languages, or more specifically, in Francophone Creole languages of the Antilles, which have almost completely broken away from French. We are in the presence of a large variegated pattern of precipitations and transformations. Do we accept colonization as an acquired fact? If we fight against it, does it not still bear an irreversible influence? The very phenomena of colonization gradually make it so that one can use a language without ever having known a foundational episode in that language: Roncesvalles is neither transportable nor exportable as a constitutive episode. Have oral languages known foundational episodes? We'll avow our – possibly temporary – ignorance. But we still ask the question.

The event which Quebec would probably consider constitutive is the final defeat of Montcalm against the British,* which determined the domination of Anglophone Canada and the subsequent resistance. Let's remember that the epic likes defeat. The Quebec epic of infinite spaces. However, the notion develops that language is not constitutive of Being. The ontological aspect is displaced from a unicity of language to a diversity of situations: the language of Quebec begets joual, and creolized languages vary in a limitless fashion. A new way of considering Being appears today, not as an exclusive or even as a pure consecutiveness, but as what I call Relation, a diversity: an ordering and a consciousness of the ever-moving relationships in and with the world.

A.L. A question arises naturally from what you have just said: I was going to ask you what the relation was between your work and epic. Let's start out by considering that *epos* comes from the Greek *epain*, which quite simply means 'utterance'.

É.G. We may consider epic as the first attempt at writing History, of writing or enunciating an epoch. To this extent, we may consider the great foundational books that I have just mentioned decisive. In the beginnings of those communities that I have been discussing, it would almost be impossible to conceive of a means of expression other than the epic. To begin with, this

---

* Louis-Joseph de Montcalm-Grozon (1712–59) was a military commander who led the French forces in North America against the British during the Seven Years' War. He was killed at the Battle of the Plains of Abraham.

is because it is about 'enunciating' an era, or in other words, beginning to stammer out a History. I say 'stammer' because consciousness is naïve, and not yet political. Next, it is a stammering because all foundational books, absolutely all of them, constitute the beginning of a writing from oral traditions. Whether we're talking about *The Song of Roland* or Icelandic sagas, there exists at the beginning narrated stories which have not yet entered into History, which are then totalized, resumed, and written to constitute the substance of epic books. As a result, epic has two characteristics: epic is the stammering of History by a naïve consciousness, but it is also the written representation of oral tradition. It is at the stage of orality that one or more stories are narrated; conversely, when the written score functions, the epic text no longer simply narrates, it speaks, and literature appears underneath, unlike the 'oral literature' of the Haitians.

So these two aspects challenge me deeply, to the point of absurdity: on the one hand, for me as for so many others, the task is not to resume or transcribe oral traditions, but to get back to orality by means of a writing that has been exposed to us, that we have been taught. What is missing for us today, and what has been missing for such a long time, is the content of the oral tradition. This tradition is what we used to find and reconstitute by means of the written word, most often by going from one language to another. But in doing this we changed the writing, which is to say that we reinvented the oral drive present in all writing, without having to tell stories. We began the epic anew. To enunciate: the world.

On the other hand, we have the second facet of this epic, which is the stammering of History. The contemporary communities which I am discussing are not without history, but are without a firm historical memory because of the ravages and effacements of colonial activity, which did not affect China, India, and Japan, or at least not as far as historical memory is concerned. So now we have to plumb this memory once again. The trap would be attempting to do so by means of a directive political conscience. Quite often, political conscience in the West, which has imposed it upon us, is a partisan conscience, and the political party is not conscience. The partisan stance is that which sets and sometimes militates within consciousness. This has been taught to at least half of the peoples of the world. Literary work, or at least mine, absolutely joins up with the concerns of epic, but with a twist. We are no longer tasked with stammering History, but with finding lost, untellable stories. It is not about resuming oral traditions in writing, but rather, about plumbing the written in order to, by means of the written word, recover and cut deeper into the utterances of these oral traditions. It's the same pathway, but in reverse. But neither does it entail politically managing the epic (as Berthold Brecht wanted?): historical naïveté is here mediated by the instinctive innocence of the poet. The epic, along with the tragic, are general conditions for the exposition of assembled and globalized modern literatures.

We have to dig a little. This is because the laws of epic such as they have been manifested in the Western world, for example, cannot be operable for us; neither can the laws of the tragic, from which the necessity for a sacrificial hero emerged. The laws of epic exclude political consciousness. Plato, who despised epic and myth, was the one who brought political consciousness into ancient Greece with his exposition or philosophical scheme of the city, and after him, Aristotle, with his views on the necessity of the sciences. Original epic did not incorporate the lyric as such, but was a collective and intrepid form of work.

All of these conditions are no longer ours; we have already undergone political consciousness, and have experienced lyrical, personal, individual expression. We have also overcome the necessity of the sacrificial hero. These are conditions that no longer befit us, but they do not keep epic form from being the one that we must investigate and work with now. And this, not because of our defeats, but because of our recoveries. According to what Hegel says about the epic, its function is to reassure all communities emerging –and threatened (by defeat). We must tie that into political conscience, without that same conscience in turn threatening from the inside. Our nascent community, so deeply endangered, is what is and will be the Whole-World. Modern epic speaks its whispered conscience and word.

A.L. This return to orality strikes me profoundly because I see in it a noteworthy similarity to the medieval cleric (a circumstance probably at work in *The Song of Roland*) who learns to read and write a cultured, artificial language – which is Latin – and who must return to orality, which I would call the native language in this specific case, to compose the French text. Isn't there a remarkable comparability of situation to what you have just described?

I had a second question, which I'll ask here. In speaking about epic and the epic project, we have completely ignored the question of myth, which is a different matter. What distinguishes myth from epic, as well as from the Old Testament, is exactly what you have called the historical conscience which stammers at its beginnings.

É.G. We can set up a difference between myth and epic, that's for sure. But I think that myth and epic both respond to the same function. In myth, and in an unconscious way, the task was to reassure the community about its existence in the world. It is for this reason that we have distinguished, for example, between foundational myths, which respond to this function, and operational myths. Operational myths are those that resume and paraphrase the techniques of communal life: how to hunt, how to contend with climatological rigors, how to construct habitations, how to get married, how to constitute families, a society. Foundational myths, more obscure, respond to the question, 'Where do we come from?': creation of the world, genesis, expansion of societies. All of them do it indirectly, and the significance of myth is always deferred. Modern literatures dating from William Faulkner have rediscovered this art of deferment. Should we say that myth only becomes legible when a community's history has confirmed its obscurities? In Greece, what creates the link between myth and epic is the Olympus of the gods, the explanation, motivation, and reason of History. If we hesitate to interpret the great African myths, it is simply because we hesitate in our knowledge of this continent's histories and their meanings.

What is the tragic? Ultimately, it is the moment when the representation of the myth has been made visible for the community. Not only are stories told, but they are also staged, with a poet who plays an instrument, sings, recites, and dances. The text is already set: the tragic is the crystallization of myth. It is the moment when the myth becomes interpretable. As with epic, what tragedy contributes in its relation to myth is the stammering conscience of History. Very generally, and even if myth develops temporal periods, it is not yet susceptible to dating: to the contrary, even when the tragic speaks about very ancient times, it is addressing the present. Whereas myth cannot summon up a present time while simultaneously plumbing the depths and the chasms. From myth to the epic and the tragic there is no essential distance: it is simply a difference of style, of staging and representation, at least for Western civilizations and civilizations occurring particularly around the Mediterranean. And if the meaning of myth is deferred, the significance of epic is divided (it speaks, for example about real defeats in terms of victories), and that of tragedy is veiled (which is why we understand the mechanism of tragic action as an unveiling, the resolution of the dissolute).

Now let's turn to the example of pre-Columbian peoples – the Aztecs, Mayas, Incas – and the books that they wrote, the *PopolVuh* and the *Chilam Balam*. These are mythic works, but were most often written after colonization, immediately after colonization. They are also historical books. We can see in these works that they will not stammer History, because History is already there and is already a defeat. These books will brandish myth as a means to equip the collectivity against the defeat that History has already accomplished. As a result, there will be no progression of the sort that occurs in countries of the Western world, as when myth proceeds to the tragic (tragedy resuming myth, exemplified by the Oedipal myths and others that are recovered by tragic theatre), and then from the tragic and epic to the lyric (from Homer to Hesiod, etc.,) and finally from the lyric to the romance (such as the Greek and Latin romances). There is a *succession of objects and projects*, and a diversification of genres is established. But with respect to pre-Columbian peoples, this work was not done because myth was immediately dissolved in the suffering consciousness of historical defeat. For that matter, in cultures of creolization, born generally out of processes of colonization, stories constitute myth and epic while defying and distorting them, signalling that the history of the community is not (yet) liberated.

Myth strikes at the unconscious in a deaf way, whereas epic poetry addresses a national consciousness not yet sure of itself. Still, the entirety of a community's knowledge is already withheld in the stammering of epic consciousness. I think it important to say and repeat this difference. In *The Iliad* or *The Song of Roland*, we have the emerging consciousness of Greece or France, each considered as a relation (or future nation); it is no longer the abyss of myth. Myth does not engage with temporality, is not constitutive of time, and does not recognize the consecutive. It reassures the collectivity, but does not announce the nation.

A.L. Which is why we find, with uncanny regularity, the same myths in extremely different populations.

É.G. Because the concrete dimension of a population *is not* implied at the level of myth. The multiplicity of myth does not attest to a generalizing universality, but instead takes stock of Relation, which disperses itself in the manner of a spreading root.

A.L. So if I may extrapolate, the question of nationhood is strongly linked to an emergence out of myth. The power of the simulacrum plays very well in epic poetry. I'll give you an example that I intend to develop a little further on: Saracens are in no way monotheistic Muslims, but pagans who adore idols. At the conclusion of *The Song*, in invaded Saragossa, Charlemagne has the idols destroyed and says: 'Now Christian law has been established'. I interpret this gesture in the following way: replacing the idol that he has destroyed, Charlemagne has himself assumed the position of the idol. He is the secret idol of *The Song of Roland*.

What interests me most in this double gesture of explicit destruction but also implicit construction is that the role of the simulacrum is fundamental in the constitution of a community. The simulacrum or the idol is that which binds, that which assembles, that which makes the community homogeneous. It is fascinating to see this function at work in *The Song of Roland*. The question that I would ask you is this: does not the idea of community rely on the power of the simulacrum?

É.G. What relies on the simulacrum is indeed the idea of community, but community such as we have lived or experienced it up until the present. Moreover, we could establish a link between what you have called the simulacrum, which is sometimes invisible, and the real integrative power of the totem, which is always spectacular.

Still, if we consider the idea of every present-day community as a community inseparable from its relation to others, meaning other communities, then the simulacrum loses its force, as does the totem. This is because the simulacrum is the isolation and consecration of a unique root. One cannot create a simulacrum of a spreading root, a rhizome (the term here is taken from Deleuze and Guattari). A unique root, or taproot, can have a simulacrum made of it and can be totemized. One can even make a simulacrum of a community if that community considers itself supreme, relieved of all relationship and all consequence. But if the community considers itself a community among others, the simulacrum cannot be practiced as it would have no aim. An epic poem such as *The Song of Roland*, which, as you have understood, is a *bearer of simulacrum*, would be impossible to conceive today. We could only suggest caricatures of it. This is how the Nazis caricaturized the epic work of Wagner, who perhaps gave them a little assistance.

A writer today conjectures his work in a language, but in the presence of all the languages in the world. And this was not the case just a short while ago. What do we mean by this? We do not mean that the writer speaks all of the world's languages. Nor do we mean that he speaks two or three or four languages. He can speak only his language and write only in his language. But he writes in the presence of all of the languages in the world: even if the writer knows and practices only his language, the totality of languages shows up and haunts him. This is an altogether new situation. Multilingualism is no longer simply a convenient way of dealing with others; multilingualism is becoming a way *not to be monolingual in the language that one uses*, a new constitutive dimension of Being in the world. In the appearance of Western languages (Romance and Saxon, and the great vernacular languages that developed from them), a transcendental process developed, a process of the passage from oral to written.

We found ourselves in a reverse situation: the great written languages, the vernacular languages and languages of transcendence, are more and more brought into the presence of the ancient tongues of orality that they dominate and which, in turn, made their appearance on the great stage of the world along with the terrible problems of the passage from oral to written. These are problems which the great vernacular languages had already resolved, but resolved at the time of their aggregation on the basis of a slow process. From this, we can see the importance of the widely extended time range that I have mentioned, the slow process that was not contradictory in that its contradictions were not painfully and tragically experienced. Today, an opposite trajectory is being brought about: we no longer proceed from oral to written, but we are passing from a situation of unique transcendence of the written to a situation of relativizing, concerning these languages. And for several reasons: first, the audiovisual is disarticulating the transcendental mass of writing in vernacular languages. We may well wonder if literature as the space of writing will not soon be a deserted, or at least, weakened space. Second, we may consider the appearance of oral languages, which no longer need to accomplish a slow and transcendental advance toward writing: they enter into the immediate process of writing, with all the contradictions that come up against them. This is the case not only for oral languages, but also for a number of written languages such as Chinese (consider the 'Romanizing' of Chinese writing). These processes, immediate and dramatic, include no progressive temporal ranges, and are sometimes accomplished by fits of decree: the new writing of Chinese has been imposed. In the matter of languages, we are witnessing a dynamic opposite to the one that developed, for example, in the Middle Ages. Linguistic fragilities are today immediately fatal, their death struggles brief, and their thunderings foundational.

The conclusion of this can only be the following: when we have a conception of Being that supposes overcoming the avatars of History (and which postulates, for example, the simultaneous presence of everyone to all of the histories of mankind, with no exception), language is then comprised in the inextricability of languages; it is no longer considered essentially or absolutely constitutive of Being.

Let's tell it like it is: this means that today no one can claim: 'Tell me which language you speak ...', because the ontological field of election of language does not coincide in any sort of discriminate or selective way with the field of the world's communities defined by their historical divisions.

It seems to me that this is the big difference between these time periods, our own and the European Middle Ages (and which leads us, paradoxically, to see or fantasize our era as a global Middle Ages, undoubtedly because we hope for future Renaissances). And yet this difference supposes for these two epochs the same reference to the absolute, to which all humanities seem to be attached. Now, for modern peoples, couldn't the absoluteness of Being be sketched out as an entire Relation, a total admitted diversity, instead of being imposed as a dramatic unicity, sundered by tensions between a Truth and its heresies, as that unicity has been lived in, say, the European Middle Ages?

A.L. My reading of *The Song of Roland* is deeply influenced by the poetics of Relation, in that I think that the cleric does not simply record a datum, but goes further to invent something, that being the nation-state of the future. And you have made an essential remark: this has to occur through a poetics, an enunciation.

This operation is at work both in *The Oaths of Strasbourg*,* to which you have alluded, and in *The Song of Roland*, a foundational work, in a different form. In both of these there is an act in the language, an enunciation which gives birth to a new political state.

É.G. I agree in every respect. It occurred exactly like that. Yes, it occurred in that way. Both of us have said it.

And it can no longer happen like that. We're dealing with two different things. I completely agree that up until the nineteenth century in the West we could reasonably venture: 'Tell me what language you speak ...' Creative investigation of the literary work was not practiced ahead of the language

---

* The Oaths of Strasbourg were a statement of allegiance between Louis the German and his half-brother Charles the Bald, made in 842. They are written in three different languages: Medieval Latin, Old Gallo-Romance and Old High German, and are often seen as the earliest surviving written evidence of a Romance language.

in this case, but after it. *The Song of Roland* is a good example. It lays the foundation for the nation and it is the nation to come.

But when the world exploded and made itself obvious as a finally realized totality, language was no longer the imperious schoolmaster of the written form for whatever fundamental idea of the world that was in question. The diverse then refashions language and proposes other adventures for it.

Literature no longer functions in the same way as, shall we say, a literature functions. There are literary works that have announced not the constitution of language, the initiation of its power, but its relativizing, as with James Joyce. These literary works have forged ahead. *The Song of Roland*, in the aftermath of its writing and through it, announced the constitution of a nation and a language, threading its way through the allure of the empire which it authorized. In the same way, Joyce's work is ahead of the relativizing of language, announced it and authorized it; his work illustrates language and leads to its ritual sacrifice (meaning, entirely literary), undoubtedly in order to change the language, or then to switch languages, as freely as possible. The grandeur of languages is for us in the change and exchange, not in an immobile reflection.

A.L. *Ulysses* is thus an epic in reverse.

É.G. In reverse, yes, but it is an epic which speaks about defeats as all epics do, even though the hero of *Ulysses* is in no way epic or heroic. His wandering throughout Dublin is a long series of bewildering solitudes. (In terms of change and exchange, the share of languages of orality is massive and decisive.)

The general course of literature has been radically altered in the 20th century. Formerly, at least in Europe, it aimed to set up the strict relation of languages, the human, and nation-states, and even the strict relation of language to Being. The literary work today grows out of a space that is not yet defined: perhaps it will be planet Earth (as McLuhan tried to show). It grows out of an inextricability in which all languages will need each other, despite situational hegemonies.

Let's suppose this: in a place that will be planet Earth, multirelation to this space will not occur, as one might think, through the practice of a universal language such as, for example, Anglo-American, but instead through the overall activation of multiple languages, and the activation of languages in Being. I am in agreement with the vision that you have developed (an enunciation that gives rise to a state), but only if we consider that it is an altogether historical vision, no longer valid today. Enunciation today enlightens and heralds, not a new political state, but a heretofore unknown relation.

Dominated languages, or languages that die out, or languages of creolization, or languages tragically quartered in folklore – might we not conceive that they could take on another project, *a poem born out of something*, which would rally epic instinct in a poetics of the multiplicity of languages? There indeed, that would be the contemporary equivalent of what you call, and I'm in agreement with it, 'an act in language'.

A.L. Do you posit or propose a primacy of political and economic structures in relation to, say, a literary entity? Or not at all?

É.G. Certainly not, I am in no way infatuated with that sort of absolutism. I think that the discussion is quite out of date, that European intellectuals of forty or fifty years ago have worn it out. It was also a time before anticolonial struggles had broadened the panorama of this discussion. For example, the notion of an international proletariat was very quickly overridden, along with its systems of domination.

Once again, no. If, for example, I have alluded to real towns and farms in the Middle Ages, to the forms of government and social organization that followed from them, it was to underscore that these societal transformations were ultimately fairly slow. The Roman farm lasted for a long time, cities imposed their own *permanence*, and the evolution of languages was likewise very progressive, in that languages appeared very quickly but were slowly transformed. The broadened temporal span is propitious, so that speech and the city grow together, without the triggering of any mechanism of priority or primacy. These lengthy delays in process would be impossible to sustain today. Time is overtaking human societies, and they are well aware of it.

A.L. During the time that we are discussing, Gallo-Roman villas were becoming larger and larger. There were billionaires before, during, and after the invasions.

É.G. Throughout Gaul, they had the status of Roman senators. If I emphasize this relation, it is to say how the very slowness of the social transformation was the same as (and accompanied) the slowness of the appearance and transformation of new languages. These were not cataclysmic phenomena. Moreover, we may note that invasions are most often cataclysmic in terms of killings and genocides, but they may not be so in terms of disintegration. Structures remain: examples are the Roman farm, the appearance of *suburbs*, the appearance of towns, which are the forerunners of cities, marketplaces, and fairs that last for centuries on end. Certain fairs in present-day Europe are the inheritors of medieval fairs. Temporal spans are so consecutive (invaders are absorbed) that, even if the processes of constitution of languages were not uniform, they were still not perceived as dramatic. Languages thus evolved without traumatizing.

Disruptions of languages today are dramatic, instantaneous, and terrifying. Evolutions are vertiginous as well, and evolutions just as dumbfounding as they are ephemeral. There will no longer be room to consider linguistic fields as analyzable and unconditionally predictable. Linguistics as a science will perhaps become an art, with the human sciences soon redeployed as Arts of the human. Multiplicity and inextricability would then enter into knowledge, in the same way that chaos theory has entered the domain of physical sciences.

A.L. We must thus oppose the phenomenon of invasion to the phenomenon of colonization. If I'm following you on this point, invasion is brutal, but its effects are slow and reciprocal on invader and invaded alike. Colonization, on the other hand, is rapid, and its effects are also very rapid, but perhaps less definitive, less radical, except for the benefits derived by the colonist.

É.G. In invasion, after massacres, there is profound and mutual transformation, with a creolization forming in a new naturalness. In colonization, after the massacres of conquest, there is a painful and unilateral mutation only of the colonized, whether they resist or not. The colonizer remaining on site will have a tendency to consider the more or less docile colonized persons as a simple given of the situation. But they change as well, without really knowing it: creolizations catch up with them in the end.

A.L. We have set aside the primacy of the economic, or of the infrastructure over the superstructure. This leads us to another question: in your opinion, is language a structuring force, or not? In other words, with the displacement that you have noted, from invasion to colonization, is the problematic of languages posed in different terms?

É.G. If we consider that there is Being above all else, then language is structuring, and this is obvious when we examine what has happened in the course of the histories of western cultures. But if we consider that Being is not primordial, and that what is constitutive (to be very brief) is not Being but instead Relation, then by the same token language will not be in and of itself constitutive. Exchanged language follows invasion, traumatized language follows colonization. The relation between two or several languages can contribute to Being. One and the same language can branch out into many different ones. Language is thus a constitutive force only in its relation to other languages. If language is constitutive in and of itself, it is so only in a closed, and often aggressive, manner. If a language is constitutive in relation to other languages, it is so in a nonaggressive, participatory, sometimes mischievous and sometimes hidden way, in spite of the violence of the encounter and their strange tearings.

Societal clashes do not decide the end of Relation, nor do they trigger its renewal. Relation is a poetics of the inextricable, not a happy ending story.

A.L. If I may resume, the barbarian is that person on the outside who does not know how to speak well. An interesting thing in the tradition that I have studied is that the rhetoricians of Latinity, for example, always insist upon correction. They have an 'Attic' point of view about language. Language must obey rules that have been framed across history. But the writer is exempt from these rules: he can commit barbarolexies, aesthetic 'faults' against the rules of eloquence, which in turn become rules and models of expression. Here, literature has a very specific function in that the writer is the one who puts the exteriority of the barbarian into language and into the rules of language. So my question is the following: today, haven't being barbarian and being correct become something else? Does not being barbarian imply that one cannot or can no longer hear the rustling of the world's languages?

É.G. Linguistic controls of the period not only protected the domain of language itself. Without doubt, these rules existed to protect not only language and its exposition, but also the entirety of culture and civilizations which exemplified them. In the same way, under slavery, the master prohibited the slave, under penalty of death, from learning how to read and write. In other words, syntactic rule had a very clear metalinguistic usage. The barbarian was the one who didn't speak the language. But let's remember that, little by little, and here is where the importance of time spans comes in, he invests this language. Roland or the Normans are Christianized. They learn the language. Of course, they introduce exogenous terms, many of which have passed into the language, but their mission is to protect the entirety of their culture against other barbarians, those who have not yet come into it. Normans of the Seine protected this part of Gaul against Normans of the Loire, who didn't know how to speak the language and who were still pagan. Here we see the integrative function of the language, aimed at better defending the language and better preserving the culture.

Today, it seems that the interest of the world's cultures is no longer simply to preserve themselves. The interest or question of the world's cultures is knowing how to participate in the blending of the world's cultures without losing themselves in it. The answer: it is necessary to be, all at once, oneself, the other, and *one other*. This is also valid for language. Brutally changing language is the exploit of a rebel, orchestrating this change appears revolutionary. Language no longer has to protect itself in an obvious and extremist manner. Instead, it wants to try to engage artfully with the world: in other words, to preserve itself as an idiom, and, at the same time, to deploy itself in as many of the world's receptacles as possible. To my way of thinking, this is the calling of the writer, to assume as much as possible responsibility for this radiant bursting. In all languages (and whatever conception of language they may have had), writers represent the force that affirms language while questioning it. This function, which was difficult when the language was only a language that protected itself, is becoming all-consuming today, because no language today can totally protect itself. Exhibiting the language while transcending it within its very interior, and on the horizon of the world – this is perhaps the trembling design of today's writer. It is not only a function of the exercise and production of language, but above all of the practice and questioning of global civilizations. Illuminating a 'new' language or illustrating a threatened language is thus contributing to the world. You are so right to underscore the point: the barbarian, wherever he may be found, is now the one who does not understand this (he does not see the world), or who does not want to admit it.

♦ 5 ♦

'Revealing the constants of global Relation'

Alexandre Leupin. It is clear that we need to address the question from the perspective that literature creates names, new names for new things, and that through poetry it influences our structuration of reality.

Here I refer to Lacan: 'Truth proves itself in a structure of fiction'. This statement, which separates fiction from any conception of simplistic deceit, gives to the study of literature, of fiction as a whole, the fullness of its significance. Without this enunciation, literature is only a meaningless idle tale. For example, Rousseau invents the 'noble savage': if we scan modern media, we find the noble savage everywhere. This concept has a decisive importance in the foundation of disciplines such as ethnography, anthropology, and other sciences of man that you call the Humanities.

Édouard Glissant. I would like to return to this role of poetry and literature, to what it can be in our current world given the fact that we have been brought up on Western literature (we have to admit that we don't know very much about Chinese, Indian, Japanese, or other literatures; we have scarcely begun to know that they exist, and how they exist). To say it roughly, (and this view requires nuance), all the effort, drive, and tension of Western literature is allied to the concept of Being as Being. With the exception of heresies, it seems to me that all occidental literatures have gone in search for Being as Being. This is to say that all occidental literatures are associated with a quest for depth. It is only in extreme and violently reactive moments among poets that forms of baroque literature, for example, appear, and these are not literatures of depth, but are what I would call literatures of breadth. I believe that we can recuperate the dimension of this search for depth in its best expression when we have recourse to the thought formulated by Lacan. But that said, Lacan places himself in the perspective of Being as Being. And this is where it seems that we have a point to question. If literature continued being connected to a search of Being as Being ('the truth'), it would no longer be important in the prevailing sentiment of the actual world. In Western civilization, haven't we already renounced literature and art, for the sake of pursuing something else? Aren't we simply following along through mechanism and habit? Haven't these Western cultures and civilizations, if not understood, at least suspected that the search for depth and the question of Being as Being are to be dismissed in favour of something else? But what? For example, in favour of a technological investigation of the world, or of many other dimensions linked to technological fields and to the absolute quest for freedom of profit. In certain Western cultures, these pursuits can make it seem that literature is useless, or in any case, hardly probable. This is how it would be if literature and poetry had to continue being linked to the search for Being as Being.

Yet literature and poetry today have dimensions not of a language or of a nation, but of global Relation. Considering this, we can abandon the ambition of Being as Being and everything associated with it, namely, a search for a depth, a plunge into an unknown or an abyss, which, as Lacan proposes, only (a) fiction can verify. Instead, we can conceive of literature as a linking, a setting in relation. In other words, as the unique dimension of humanity that can capture, and reveal, the constants of global Relation. If literature is a search for depth, if it must be answerable to a theory of Being as Being, we can indeed think, or at least globally or collectively suspect, that it would no longer be necessary as we approach the world's contradictions. I do wonder if this belief isn't at work in Western cultures today. But if literature is a quest for the invariable, a clarification of the fundamental ideas of global Relation, then it continues to be of a human dimension, in the Western world as elsewhere, and elsewhere as in the Western world: it's not surprising that non-Western peoples have more confidence in poetry than occidental people do. As is spuriously proposed, this is because they need the positioning in global Relation. New on the world stage, their imaginary is at ease in this dimension of relation. And this is why literature – in South America, Brazil, the Caribbean, in Africa, Asia, and in countries that have not peddled universality, and in all diasporas – has perhaps a more instrumental status than it now does in European countries. Without doubt, this is only a transitory stage.

The second proposal that I wanted to submit is that we need to beware here of nominalism. In other words, we should not let ourselves think that revelation is in the words or letter of the text or in speech. I think that the letter of the text or of speech withholds the possibility for the imaginary to form or reform itself. That is what is in the text. But it is not reality, as has been believed in the West. As for story tellers, who accumulate pseudo-models of transparency or deciphering, the world's impenetrability can only wear them out across time.

So in this case, what do we call it: Relation?

We do not name Relation, inextricably because it is not nameable.

Why is it unnameable?

It is unnameable because it is unpredictable. Nowhere should we set our sights at reaching the innermost reality principles of global Relation, as that would be a futile project. In Western literatures, we have always tried to advance by a plunge into depth: a plunge into the real, as far as the truth of the real. Western science has also assumed this attempt, going as far as the atom, which until recently was considered the ultimate reality underneath appearances. From the perspective of what I call global Relation, this attitude, this option, this preoccupation fall by the wayside because Relation has no reality principle; it only has principles of relation. What shows up in the light of the text is not the real as such, nor the real allegedly *propounded* by the fiction (as fiction never propounds anything but *its own idea* of the real), but the constants that are inscribed in the innumerable intricacies of this real, which at the same time constitute it. Various states of the world. I believe that literature and poetry meet or discover there a new existential function, which they have nevertheless always upheld. As a result, I think that we need to return to the time of the pre-Socratic poet-philosophers: multiplying contacts and intuitions to avoid the Truth that strangles and kills.

A.L. I was thinking not so much about nominalism as about the effects of the literature that we are discussing. Let's admit that there would now be a literature which is no longer a literature of meaning, but of Relation, and I do not mean a senseless relation. This is where you are constituting a structure that will have effects. If I have understood, the difference here would be that this structure would create readers who, in their own turn, will be unpredictable.

É.G. What a beautiful idea! But also, such a structure addresses readers who will no longer accept verifying in it only a principle of reality, but who, through the detour of this structure, will think themselves capable of truly imagining a principle of relation. It's not the same thing. A literature of meaning is not in every case a literature of the real, and Relation is indifferent to the finality of meaning – it is up to us to furnish that. But we shouldn't propose that readers themselves would be unpredictable, any more than we should note or hope that they would be of *the happy few*. The very object of Relation is unforeseeable, but the structure of a work does not take into account the reader's unpredictability. No literature today claims to descend into the depths down to a principle of reality, as science formerly did in plumbing the depths of the real. All literatures tend (should claim, or must, if need be, claim, or could claim, without obligation) to extend themselves in scope out to a principle of relation.

These are just so many peremptory declarations which do not amount to authoritative principles intended to rule literature. Simply put, we sometimes need to push our radicalisms to the limit, stiffly confirming our lines of flight or evasion, so that afterwards we may together forget the whole of it (meaning all of this categorical talk), when the articulation of the poem is there.

✦ 6 ✦

'Separating from the place of speech, the better to return to it'

Alexandre Leupin. What has struck me in medieval literature, but also in many others, is that, contrary to what the positivist critical tradition believed, discourse only occurred at the expense of a separation from the place of enunciation, of an identity in the imaginary, of a social reality. Here, two brief examples: at the end of the first poetic text in French literature, *The Canticle of St. Eulalia*,* the dove of the Holy Spirit separates itself from the body of the saint. This dove of the Holy Spirit is also the breath of poetic inspiration of the French language, and there is a cleaving from the locus of martyrdom, the real place of the saint who in fact represents the very possibility of poetic evolution. Another example, this time taken from Provençal literature, is the famous poem by William IX of Aquitaine,** in which he says that he is composing a poem about or out of pure nothingness; in this way, he pegs as a source of his speech something which is, literally speaking, nothing. So from these two brief examples (but which could be found elsewhere) I deduce an axiom, which is that literature *exists only* if it is torn away from its place of origin, from the determinations that weigh upon it, while reinventing those same determinations in its structure. This process then leads back to the point of departure, where literature, having withstood a kind of anamorphosis or metamorphosis, finds itself at once modified and modifying. I think

---

* *The Canticle of Saint Eulalia* – also known as the *Sequence of Saint Eulalia* – is the earliest surviving piece of hagiographical writing in France. Written around 880, it is also one of the earliest surviving texts written in the vernacular langues d'oïl (or Old French).

** William IX was the Duke of Aquitaine and Gascony between 1086 and his death in 1127. Celebrated for his political and military achievements, he is best known as the earliest troubadour (a lyric poet in the Occitan language) whose work has survived.

that a large part of what you have done responds to this experience of departures and returns.

Édouard Glissant. I have called this movement the practice of detour, particularly among the peoples of the Caribbean. It is astonishing how Caribbean intellectuals (and I'm not only speaking of poets) have become interested and involved in problems raised elsewhere, among other peoples. For example, Marcus Garvey,* a Jamaican, practically took over the problems of Black Americans, and further, among these Black Americans, a great number of leaders and movements come from the Caribbean, from Jamaica, Trinidad, or Barbados. There are other famous examples, such as Fanon in Algeria, or Césaire who considers an overall return to African authenticity, or George Padmore,** from Trinidad to Ghana. During this time of world discovery, we see a sort of extraversion among the Antilleans, perhaps because the Antilles are an archipelago, a procession of active and extinct volcanoes, where the wind rules.

Now I will speak about the opposition between the Mediterranean and the Caribbean Sea. I think that the Mediterranean – and this is its historic greatness – is a sea that concentrates. It's not happenstance that the greatest monotheistic religions of the world emerged on the hills, in the cities, and in the deserts that surround its banks. It is a sea centred on the One, which maintains in its surrounding regions the multiplicity of the diverse, tragically inclining that multiplicity toward this oneness. It is a sea of fundamental chasm, of an internal abyss that determines all philosophies of the One. I think that places where the sea does not concentrate, but instead diffracts, where the movement of explosion is quite pronounced and where the wind seems to blow naturally from everywhere and in all directions, I think that these places are propitious for the emergence of a philosophy of the naturalized diverse. For an aesthetics of the detour. This is the case with the Caribbean archipelago.

But this is not the only reason why I am remarking on the practice of detour. Detour is at the very source of all literature. The literary

---

* Marcus Garvey (1887–1940) was a Jamaican publisher, journalist and political activist. Founder of the Universal Negro Improvement Association and African Communities League, he was a prominent pan-Africanist whose own ideas were gathered under the term Garveyism.
** George Padmore (1903–59) was born Malcolm Nurse in Trinidad. He was a leading figure in the communist and pan-African movements. Toward the end of his life he moved to Ghana, where he was an adviser to President Kwame Nkrumah.

work which does not turn itself over to deviation is nothing but a literal transcription of the real. Even during the times when literature was considered to have the aim of reproducing the real as faithfully as possible, in this absolute mimesis, there was still an overstepping, an overtaking. This practice of deviating, which is at the true source of all literary work, is more profoundly evident during certain epochs. I think that the Middle Ages is one of these epochs. This is primarily because it is the time when the very notion of nationhood and the very consciousness of language are beginning to form, but are not yet dominating or restrictive. It is also the time when, as if by echo, the thought of wandering arose.

With regard to these questions, I would remind you that during the Middle Ages, we can detect many elements demonstrating that the period was very much 'in advance' over ours. For example, cooperation was beginning between Jewish and Arab philosophies, as was spiritual and didactic exchange between universities in Florence, Bologna, Paris, London, Salerno and many other places; exchanges, fairly often heretical in their extremes, also took place between monasteries in Ireland or in Germany. This movement is unquestionably pre-national, practically ignoring the emerging demands of the states and nations which will later fortify themselves; it is a movement which intensely challenges the structures and limits of knowledge. In my view, we see in this movement evidence of a deliberation about wandering, and at the same time, a search for unity. These are consequently dialectical spaces, in which the poignancy of the drama that we have evoked is set. Historically speaking, whenever a situation of transition or birth (and not rebirth, because the Renaissance is already a determination) occurs in the world, concerning either states or communities, countries or nations, philosophies, or new religions, this thinking about wandering is in force. Wandering is not rambling or divagation, as we have seen in the two examples you have cited. The poem of Saint-John Perse ('A great poem born out of nothing') in the volume *Exile*, repeats the gesture of William IX. The other day, inspired by your remark, I evoked modern epic literatures which would assume the ultimate risk of a poem *born out of something* (or of 'all things').

Let's not forget the founders of the great religions, who were themselves wanderers. It is clear that Moses, with his people fleeing from Egypt, Christ, with his apostles throughout the world, Muhammad, with his companions of the Hegira, and Buddha, along with the disciples whom he renounced, are all wanderers. In any event they live within the thinking of wandering. So what is that, the thinking of wandering? It is to leave or depart from the place that has been given to you in order to understand or live with it better. In this regard, literature accomplishes a function close to that of the great foundational projects of religions, namely, to magnify the thinking of wandering (in the world) and to oppose in all respects thinking of a fixed order. Thus, the assumption of wandering leads us to transfigure the ancient slave-driven uprooting from Africa without making a system of it.

When philosophies, no longer religious, become systematized, or when religions in the Western world become institutions, they do it in a weightier and more continental manner than the first impulses of religions (at their source), or than the reflections of poetic imaginaries. We will observe, whether it be Bossuet,* Hegel or Marx, a eurocentrism, which is the mark of becoming sedentary and the mother of conquest, which does not appear in William of Aquitaine and which has its centripetal equivalent neither in major emerging religious thought nor in the poems of the world.

I think that we are today in a comparable period. Not a period in which several national or religious or philosophical communities appear, but a period in which a chaotic community, which is the world community, erupts. Within such a setting it is no wonder that institutional thought is terrified. We are bearing witness to what I would call a determinate fact: rootedness thinking is also collapsing. An exception to this is the occurrence of eco-human catastrophes, irrepressible eruptions such as in war-torn Yugoslavia, for example, where we can currently observe the exacerbated return of repressed nationalists. But even these catastrophes seem like so many anomalies to us, as they no longer present themselves as capable of legitimacy. It is *the entire war* between Israel and Palestine that seems illegitimate to us. And if we think about the domination of the United States over the world, it seems in no way legitimate. A short while ago, colonization bore within itself its own site of legitimacy. There could be no legitimacy today, because the problem for all humanity, the powerful and the impoverished, the rich and the poor, is to know how to leave the place where one is in order to understand the world, and how, after having understood or believed to have understood the world, to return to that place where one always dies, either by surfeit or famine. Dominating the world is futile, as one is incapable of knowing or divining the world from that position. This is where literature can assert a profound and precious role, namely, allowing us to imagine the separation from our place of origin

---

* Jacques-Bénigne Bossuet (1627–1704) was a French bishop and theologian. He is now remembered primarily for his literary works, including a series of sermons and funeral panegyrics.

without turning that separation into an impassable chasm. Literature is a true apprenticeship of the world.

This is what I am resuming when I say that the writer is solitary and solidary. Solitary: he must live adventurously in the thinking of wandering, which is neither a collectivist nor a collective thought; and solidary: he must grow up completely in the thinking of his place. It is only through this practice of detour and return that the dialectic of Relation operates.

In truth, though, the writer is not subjugated to any duty. He illuminates his guileless and strong lucidities by the fire of an inextricability that he does not control.

A.L. So I'll throw out a question to you: you have spoken about African authenticity, and you have spoken about the possible and sometimes probable degrading of the thinking of rootedness. Thus, in my opinion you are indicating that there are false deviations (detours), or false returns which would be completely imaginary returns, let's call them lures, and that these lures can be damaging. That's how I understand it. Would you like to develop?

É.G. We could say, for example, that most colonizations from the second quarter of the twentieth century began in the form of a lure: they took place not as a function of something that was going to occur and that could have been the principle of Relation, but as a function of something that had already happened and that the West had already taught to an entire diaspora of people on earth. This is the principle of unique rootedness and the fact of the nation-state. And this is why we have been able to note the traumatizing consequences of the struggles of decolonization in Africa, for example: a decolonization which gave rise to the constitution of parodic states, parodic because they aimed for a goal that they had neither the processes nor the power to assure. They were not powerful states, but they were still supposed to exemplify connectedness and solidarity. The global furnace was thus fully stoked.

It is true that a false image of what you have called authenticity has been established, linked to the idea that we have of an essential being which we need 'to pursue'. This is the cause of ravages throughout the world, ravages of an identity that tolerates no relationship, and there will be many more. And then, on a much more common level, you find emerging categories which are the fruit of the same prejudices, such as the black man is emotional, the white man is rational .... I think that even Leopold Sédar Senghor said: 'Emotion is Negroid and reason is Hellenic'. These categories, which tend simply toward generalizations, remain deeply troubling because they cannot be broached, and also because they are derived from a unique and extremely fallacious conception of what has been called identity, according to which everything would be given all at once and would never vary.

A.L. Are we perhaps thinking of Alex Haley's *Roots*?*

É.G. *Roots* is perhaps the lure, maybe the example of what shouldn't be done. The book is about a new consciousness-raising for Black Americans, about the magnificence of memory and confirmed pride, about the attempt to reconstitute the discontinuous in the biography of the Afro-American collectivity, *and in this respect it is an irreplaceable book.*

But it also relies on a series of assumptions, all of which are linked to one same belief, namely, that there would be an essence or a purity of Afro-American Being, and any story that one tells, any fiction that one recites, or any film that one makes will take stock of it. Further, one would find this 'Being' in Africa, so it would be necessary to return there as to a preserved source, and all or nearly all people of the African diaspora in the Americas would ultimately be able to discover the African village from which their ancestors have been abducted (a site that would not have changed across time). Finally, through painstaking research, one would be able to trace back the chain of generations and reconstitute families. It's the idea (entirely Western) that filiation is in rootedness, not insofar as the usages that occur with it, but instead in the ideologies deduced from it, and that, for example, one could always recompose an indubitable lineage from filiation. This is doubly untrue.

You understand it all just as I do: through the trembling poetics of jazz, gospel, and blues, of reggaes, voodoo incantations and condomblés, built upon traces of disordered memory (which, for example, is completely absent in the *country music* of the United States, so perfectly constructed to be *valid for everybody*), and even in the unfurling of the possessed chants seen in those astonishing circuses of delirium, televised evangelical

---

* *Roots: The Saga of an American Family* is a 1976 novel written by American novelist Alex Haley. It tells the story of Kunta Kinte, an eighteenth-century enslaved African transported to North America. The book and an ABC miniseries it inspired played a major role in raising public awareness of African American history.

sermons, attended primarily by Black Americans. We are all marked by an assortment of tensions in art or in representation which hark back to original African inspiration, perhaps even more so than in grand appeals for a 'return to Africa'. And this is true despite, for example, the ideology of protestant churches and the paralyzing conformism of the morals expressed in these sorts of spectacle, along with the profiteering that result from it. As for the musical traditions of the Caribbean and the Creole Americas, they are already in sustained complicity with African music, their breeding ground. Everything is repetition and recall: here I need to repeat that it would be useless for us to decide *that literature would be this or that*, or to decide *what the function of the writer would be, or the nature of the world's unpredictabilities*. The surprise of the word is still hanging on the innocent artfulness of the poet, who leads us farther afield.

✦ 7 ✦

'The writer of today is always a future writer'

Alexandre Leupin. Your poems, essays, novels, and plays are inscribed in the traditional inspirations of literature. Their themes are recurrent. They respond to each other. But I don't believe there is an aim at totality in your work, or that your work is an everything, because nothing is everything, according to Lacan. On the other hand, there is a unity to it, there is a 'oneness', which is manifest in the writing; this has to be scrutinized in the diversity of its expressions. Moreover, it is a 'oneness' that does not need to be linked to an individual subject, but to something else.

Do you accept these distinctions between totality and unity, and do you agree with these remarks?

Édouard Glissant. One is flamboyant, whereas unity advances very humbly. It thus relates to the diversities of the world, as you yourself have suggested. It is apparent that every literary work has a project, and that, if a literary work has a project, even in its diversities, it requires unity. Now, the other problem is that, in the burgeoning and expansion of literatures in the Western world, genres gradually took shape and became distinct. But, as we may note right away, genres are not eternal; they appeared for reasons that have been analyzed and studied, beginning with lyric poetry and theatre, and then the novel as a technique of narration. Then genres became diverse, and assumed a kind of autonomy, most often as a reaction against each other. We may remember Boileau,* who couldn't tolerate that his valet read or even peddle a novel. What can this possibly mean? Let's examine other cultures and other civilizations. We find that novels exist there, in China and in Japan. We see that there are both poetry and novels. The

---

* Nicolas Boileau-Despréaux (1636–1711), usually known as Boileau, was a French poet, translator and literary critic. He is remembered primarily for his reforms of French poetry, known for his influence in upholding Classical standards in both French and English literature.

question that we should ask ourselves is the following: is a genre 'one' in and of itself? Bearing unity and totality at the same time? I think not. Is there a generalizing process such that nearly everywhere we end up with the same genres: theatre, poetry, the novel, essays, without counting, of course, philosophical and historical works? We cannot decisively say that there is a sort of universal process leading to generalized genres. So what is left for us?

This is what we may say: on the one hand, the literary work is univocal and diversified; on the other, there was, before the appearance of genres, a genre, a common trunk that in my opinion represented literature in its epic vocation. I characterize this literature, in Hegel's manner, as the exposition of a dawning community, a community not yet sure of its very existence, which feels threatened. The epic genre (and I am Hegelian on this point) is the expression of communal conscience when it has not yet become political conscience, meaning at the time when the community is not yet sure of its existence as a community. Epic literature brings peace and equilibrium into the community, just as tragedy later will be the resolution of the dissolute on the ancient stage. This means that epic literature is not exactly poetry, nor exactly a novel, nor exactly history, nor exactly politics, nor exactly myth. At the dawning of all communities (and this is practically a universal), we find foundational works such as the Old Testament, the *Iliad*, *The Song of Roland*, the *Bhagavad Gita*, the *PopulVuh* of the Amerindians (it was more toward the end), Icelandic sagas, *The Song of the Niebelungs* of the Germanic peoples, the *Kalevala* of the Finns, the *Shaka* of the Zulus (well before colonization), and others; foundational books such as these appear in every community that is emerging or defending itself. These are epic books, bearing the genre in themselves, but not submitting to the genre.

So the question on the one hand would be: are we living in a time of emerging communities? And on the other hand, are we living in a time of emerging communities not yet sure of themselves, meaning that they have not yet been submitted to the chemistry of political instigation? Can there be, or are there still stammering consciences?

It seems to me that we cannot respond positively to these two questions. If we are truly in a time when new communities are emerging, and if we are struck by the appearance of that 'hidden face' of the earth where countries of the South are found, it is still true that this emergence can only be accomplished in relation to other, already existing communities, which have themselves been submitted to political instigation in the modern sense of the term. No awareness of community emergence today can be safeguarded from the instigation of political action, which has already taken place elsewhere in space and time, and which is communicated here in either a positive or negative way.

These new communities appear in relation with existing communities, which, we'll repeat, have themselves already undergone incitement to political action. Most often, these have been communities of oppression or colonization or expansion, which have thus more often imposed rather than proposed, ruled rather than shared.

Renewed emergence today is not so much about communities as about an unexpected appeal to other modes of relationship between human communities.

What appears from now on is the real emergence of the totality-world, which has already been prey to political incitement, but which must perhaps escape it, in another direction. This other direction cannot be the naïve innocence of primitive epic. It has to be a direction which supposes the political as a dimension while overtaking the political as an injunction. In this new situation, we have to conceive a new common trunk, with Relation fanning out from it. And it is this new common trunk (which may not be an epic literature but will in any case be a literature, a reading of the world) which will integrate and go beyond all possible genres. This means that, after the extremely fertile and prodigiously illuminating moment of the specificity of genres in Western literature and elsewhere (in China or Japan, for example), this new situation requires, from the standpoint of literary techniques and expression, the new common trunk. And this trunk will not be in the image of the epic literature in the foundational books of humanity. This common trunk will knowingly and in full consciousness encompass political activation and its surpassing, the mastery of various literary genres and their undoing, the unpredictable leaps of the Whole-World and their giddiness: such a unity will not be given in advance, it is to be conquered.

And why wouldn't that also be a totality? The Whole-World is not in itself totalitarian. The good taste of a totality is that it leaves none of the world's differences by the wayside, not even the smallest particularity. At the very beginning of our conversations, following one of your remarks, I had proposed that the poem touches on everything, without being reduced to the ambition of nothingness.

This is why I have thought that we are always ethnologists of ourselves. The writer is the 'ethnologist of himself',* he integrates in the unicity of his work the entire diversity not only of the world, but also all of the world's

---

* Glissant quotes here from his own *Soleil de la conscience* / *The Sun of Consciousness*.

techniques of exposition. The surpassing of genres is thus made necessary by this new situation; in this situation, it's not really or only about expressing communities, but about expressing communities in their lively correlation to other communities. This liberates individuals and modifies the perspectives of literatures.

Literature no longer calls forth in depth an approach to Being, but would seek in breadth to reveal Relation. It relativizes in absolute terms.

This cannot be developed inside a genre, but requires the multiplication and intermingling of literary and artistic genres. Perhaps at the end of this effort, other genres will sprout and finally appear, but we have no way in the here and now of divining what they will be nor how they will engender themselves. We are striving toward them, wouldn't you say? These new genres will perhaps be born out of the integration or the effacement or the resurrection of all genres – theatre, essay, novel, poetry. Maybe we will observe extraordinary hybridities between the arts. But whatever they will be, we don't yet know. The writer of today is always a future writer.

◆ 8 ◆

'Infinitely multiplying the existence of languages'

Alexandre Leupin. The *Oaths of Strasbourg* represent a completely new act for their era (842):* the articulation of an imperial centrality, both Latin and Germanic, and peripheries, designated by the vernacular languages. In this sense the *Oaths* prefigure the nation-state defined by a specific language. What initially stands out is a function of discrimination and oppression, though it is perhaps anachronistic to speak in those terms since the human subjects assembled around the great captains owe obeisance, rather than consent, to their sovereigns, Charles the Bald and Louis the German. In order for the oath to be enforced, the sovereign does not need the consent of the vassal, who is at the lowliest level of this rowdy populace. Next, the language is shown as a substitute for an object serving feudal homage. One could make a feudal homage on a mound of earth, on all sorts of objects, even usual objects. But here, it is the language that serves as object, and this marks a very important symbolic change: swearing on and in language. On the other hand, we also see that the Latin language enunciates the other languages (Romance and Germanic) in relation to itself. This is not only a function of domination, but also pacification of the endemic confrontations in the structure of feudalism. Has this model now been superseded?

Édouard Glissant. If multilingualism does not appear necessary at the outset, it is because an individual at that time couldn't be naturally multilingual. This is why certain official texts of the Middle Ages, such as the *Oaths of Strasbourg*, are bi- or trilingual. They exist as a sort of Rosetta

---

* Glissant refers again to the Oaths of Strasbourg, a statement of allegiance between Louis the German and his half-brother Charles the Bald, made in 842. They are important as they were written in three different languages: Medieval Latin, Old Gallo-Romance and Old High German, and are often seen as a result as the earliest surviving written evidence of a Romance language.

Stone used to seal oaths. Charles the Bald swears, swearing in the language of Louis the German, so that the other's soldiers will understand him. But it is not necessarily said that the one who swears speaks the language of the other. He has perhaps learned the formula by heart. He reads a script, prepared by clerics. This practice has left us bilingual or trilingual texts which are precious for linguists. It shows us that, during this period, multilingualism was not within the scope of Being. Multilingualism is conceived only as a convenient process of transfer or translation, and not as a constitutive force of Being. Today, it seems to me that *the poetic steamboat has done an about-face*, that individuals and collectivities are credited at the outset with many feasible languages. Multilingualism is indeed for us a constitutive force of Relation.

During our current era, the idea of the centre no longer has a concrete reality. In other words, Roman power has already moved away, and now is practiced in the East. The empire of the East intervenes hardly at all in the West, perhaps in a diplomatic way, but very little in any real way. Rome is far off, or even chimerical. In a like manner the European Middle Ages will be bifurcated, composed of Roman communities in the south, and Saxon communities in the north. If I am clearly interpreting the texts that we are discussing, there is a sort of apportionment of Roman force, a throwback to the old empire, which is somehow distributed between new powers and principles, realities which will become national, but are not yet so.

If we are to speak about centre and periphery during this time, the periphery is already in the centre and shares it. The centre thus exists only as the legitimizing referent of the allotment of this real power. What is interesting is that, nearly six or seven centuries later, after Western nations have been formed and projected themselves onto the world (specifically France and England, the two most important colonial powers), they did not share a unitary imperial referent. They quarrelled about something else, which was external, outside of themselves. French and English colonial empires were built on the mode of opposition and competition: competition in Africa, competition in Asia, and before then, competition between the Portuguese and the Spanish, the French and the English in the Americas. At this time, the principle that constituted the centre, namely, the eminently superior value of Western civilizations and cultures, was not an absent standard as the Roman principle had been, absent already at the time the *Oaths* were pronounced. Instead, it was a virulent principle, still active today and in full effect, which established the legitimacy of colonizations.

What these centres quarrel about today is not their own centres, but the external, what is outside of themselves. If, at the time of the *Oaths of*

Strasbourg, the participating parties had been able to say: 'As for me, I'll take Hungary, and you, you grab the northern countries, and then I'll occupy …', and so forth all around, we would have been able to establish a parallel with situations today. If we do not consider the foundations of things, we will not see where the differences lie. So here is the difference: at the time of the *Oaths of Strasbourg*, a periphery was not defined as such, whereas during the era of colonizations, the periphery was defined as a periphery. The very notion of the ex-centric couldn't appear at the time of the *Oaths of Strasbourg*. All that could emerge was the reverential memory of the 'centred'. Everything needed to be centred as a function of the imperial Roman ideal which, though absent, still persisted as an ideal. The inconceivable notion of the off-centred accompanied that other absence, which was an unimaginable multilingualism, sequestered only in monasteries.

On the other hand, when colonizations occurred, the outlier is presented and truly defined as an outlier. One of the consequences is that endless discussions took place over whether or not Negroes had a soul, if it was legitimate to maintain them in slavery, and so forth. Then, little by little, the notion of a periphery was defined as a world-wide object. One example in French literature is when Chateaubriand utters, writes the *Itinerary from Paris to Jerusalem*.* I am not in any way proposing that Jerusalem is already considered as a periphery, but that there is already the direction of an itinerary: going from Paris toward something else. It is what could be called a directed, pointed migration, as opposed to a migration that turns upon itself, even if in Chateaubriand it is only a temporary, capricious, and non-conquering migration.

During the period that we are discussing, between 500 and 1500 A.D, it is interesting that the migrations of the Goths occur in a circle, crossing the Rhine, the Danube and the Euphrates; the Vandals, the Franks, and the Alans are involved as well. They descend, driven out by each other, dreaming of the sack of Rome. But once arrived and onsite, all of that is over, and changes. Movements of kingdoms and states are constituted in a circular manner, on the inside of the Roman centre and around the Mediterranean basin. Perhaps the directed invasions that fail, such as Attila's, are precisely those which had not envisioned the perenniality of a circular passage, of a future installation. By an opposite effect,

---

*   *Itinerary from Paris to Jerusalem* (French title: *Itinéraire de Paris à Jérusalem*) is an 1811 travel narrative by François-René de Chateaubriand. Chateaubriand set out for the Middle East in summer 1806, returning via Egypt, Tunisia and Spain in 1807.

the progression of the West upon the world and even the progression of Western thought will later be considered as sharply directed projections.

Let us note that it is also in this same sense or according to this same tendency that scientific advancement will take place: the conquests of knowledge. Only today has epistemology recognized that the advancement of sciences is not a pointed progression, but a dramatically dialectical one. From this time forth, scientific thought is sceptical of universality. Modern sciences are about chaos, and know nothing of linearity.

In colonization, there is a double notion of the centre, established not as an ideal but as a reality, and of an unknown periphery. The attempt would be to fill in the empty spaces on geographical maps, translated into legitimate properties. In this sort of advance, it seems to me that the West never, not ever, really questioned the legitimacy of its own appropriation of the world. The texts of the Enlightenment philosophers of the eighteenth century are notably impoverished in this regard. Montesquieu, Voltaire or d'Alembert sharply condemn the condition of the black man, just as Montaigne had done for the Indians, but at no time and in no texts do these Enlightenment philosophers, with the possible exception of Rousseau and Diderot, question, as Montaigne had, the legitimacy of Western appropriation of the world. What this means is that the periphery is indeed considered as the garden of the house, and not as a constitutive factor of the house itself, nor as another house to be respected. This, in my opinion, is a sharp difference. In the European Middle Ages, the rooms of the house, which was already there and already inhabited, were shared.

Here is a question: what is meant by an outlying or ex-centric way of thinking? An off-centre mindset is one which questions the legitimacy of appropriation, of extension and expansion, a way of thinking which, while informing the notions of centre and periphery, contributes to the construction of all peripheries into centres and all centres into peripheries of something else. A way of thinking which, consequently, leads to the construction of the relative element in Relation. It seems to me that one of the great conquests of the West at the time of its expansion was the approach to the notion of the absolute. The notion of the absolute is what could in turn characterize a dual way of thinking, far removed from inextricability, a mindset that conceives and legitimizes a centre and a periphery. As for the concept of the relative, of relativizing, or of relation, it is what no longer conceives centres in relation to peripheries, even if centres of economic, political or military power still exist.

In other words, it is a way of thinking which no longer considers that economic, political, or military power can be truly determinate in the very functioning of human societies, a way of thinking which no longer considers that an absolute can pre-exist all relation, a way of thinking which conceives the absolute only as the total relation of all possible relations. But the total relation which makes for the real splendour of the absolute. And here we have an important connection with what occurred in the famous *Oaths*, but a differentiated connection.

Modern poetics are no longer referenced to an ideal, Roman or not, present or absent. I translate this fact by an expression: Relation is intransitive, between all and everything.

A.L. What you have just said brings up a question: if I understand correctly, the centre and the periphery are linked to modalities of property and appropriation. So the question for our current time would be: does not everyone today, the world over, aspire to become a proprietor? What I mean is: are we not currently faced with five billion human beings who, in some way or another, frustrated by appropriation or property, still all want to become proprietors?

É.G. We can ask that question in a two-fold manner: we may conceive of a world in which every person wants to be a proprietor, because it is on these grounds that the mindset of Western absolutism would have conquered the world. (In its new ontology, a person isn't immobilized by material property, and palaces are not designed to last. A person wants to possess money victoriously, to *acquire* the most possible dollars in an almost abstract way.) And I mean if we do not count the billions of individuals expropriated by famine, epidemics, massacres, liberalized exploitation, and the ever-growing barrenness of the planet. But we may also conceive of a world in which each person could be a proprietor without seeking to establish the legitimacy of proprietary extension. It seems to me that the search for the legitimacy of the extension of property is what has marked in the most profound way (because this isn't only a negative criticism, things being what they are), and also fatal for the other, the real extension of Western property. The conqueror sought no excuses for his conquest, but instead, rights to his property. For example, if we examine Shakespeare's play, *The Tempest*, we may see it as an extremely noble attempt at legitimizing Prospero, who has the right and the power to rule over the Caribbean island of Caliban, because he is the legitimate Duke of Milan. The Duke of Milan who legitimately has the right to rule over the isle of Caliban is also endowed with the privilege of knowledge. He masters and orders the elements, serving as the depository of knowledge and change. This is one of the possible interpretations of the play (which is clearly not a tragedy, as there is no victimized hero). It has quite often put people from the periphery into question. There have been masses and masses of books, studies, analyses, and interpretations of this play. But would this legitimizing (of colonial expansion) be possible today? Even if the world aspires to be a world of proprietors, and even if, individually, these proprietors aspire to increase their property on this egocentric basis, it is still certain that this legitimizing of the collective act of appropriation cannot be sustained. If a nation, culture, or empire wants to extend itself as a power throughout the space of the world, it has to do something which was not formerly an obligation: seek the precise legitimacy of this act, whether it be found in the United Nations, or in the struggle against tyranny, or in the defence of religions, whatever you will. It will be obliged to seek out and validate an excuse. In the entire history of colonization, no Western power has ever really needed to do this. In other words, colonization naturally appeared as a legitimate expansion, necessary to the progress of the world. And this is the moment when these differences arise: at the time of colonization, the immediate outlying mindset is the way of thinking that marginalizes itself on the very inside of the centre's absoluteness, as an inheritor of the accursed thoughts of the Middle Ages. This is why I think the Middle Ages is a fascinating period, because it is during the Middle Ages, even before the era of colonizing expansions, that we see these outlying mindsets appear, tragically defend themselves, and succumb. These thoughts of the mystic and the heretic, these thoughts of the outside, the particular, and the poem's abyss, which accept neither expansion nor legitimizing, which are deployed at the very heart of the centre, live there only in hostility, and get out only through negation and sacrifice.

Fundamentally, barbarians are not the ones who represent or practice an outlying way of thinking, because barbarians fight to enter the centre so that they can profit from it. They don't fight as an imperial power fights against another imperial power, nor as a colonized land fights against a colonizer. The barbarians' desire is to cross a frontier in order to enter the centre and to be at ease in it, to take a leisurely look around. Barbarians such as these are desirous of sedentariness.

The heretic, the mystic, eccentrics, accursed poets (real nomads) are then the ones who accomplish true outlying thought. They take on as their charge the lasting power, the authentic barbarian revival.

A.L. As soon as Attila dies, the entire structure of power that he put in place falls in on itself.

É.G. The barbarian does not want to be an outlier. A truly outlying way of thinking begins with this thought from the inside, but then takes a different path from systematizing rationalism. Deviations that emerge are condemned by councils. These are outlying thoughts, on the very inside of the centre, which is already in a position to constitute itself as an absolute. To my way of thinking, outlying thoughts today come from the periphery, because they are the thoughts that question the very notions of centre and periphery and that consider the totality-world only as an infinite series of centres and an infinite series of peripheries, all in relation to each other. This is what interests me right now in the process, in the systems or non-systems of thinking at work in the world. From the standpoint of linguistic practice, this is also what makes the topic so interesting: how can languages, which are so deeply habituated to absolute centrality, become relativized as they collide with each other? We can see the importance of this question when we observe the strenuous contemporary debates over the structures of the French language. Does it need to be simplified? Does its spelling need to be simplified, and do the learning methods of the language need to be reconsidered? In any event, debates such as these don't exist for the English language, because it has spread so massively throughout the world. In its Anglo-American form it does not need to be put into question. Current examination of the French language is extremely precious, not because it is interesting in its detail (which is rather comical and incongruous), but because it translates a fairly clear anxiety, an anxiety now occurring for languages. Oral languages: should they be stabilized? If so, in what proportions, and according to which criteria? In our new situation, where there are no longer any legitimate centres or peripheries since these entities bear in themselves their own legitimacy, won't we still be (vulnerable to or) faced with a language such as Anglo-American, which will press on everywhere maintaining the notion of centre and peripheries, but in a completely univocal manner?

And in this situation, wouldn't imaginaries be in great danger of sterilization? The outlying way of thinking responds: yes, this would be a great danger for the imaginary. Anglo-American, which is the language of a nation or group of nations on the move, and which is also the language of an aggressive system of financial activities, can no longer fulfil in modernity the pacifying role that you have attributed to Latin during the Middle Ages, during that time when Latin was no longer effectively the language of the dominating and active Roman Empire, but the trace of its ideal preserved as an ideal.

Just as it is necessary to multiply incessantly centres and peripheries, so too is it necessary to multiply incessantly the existence of languages. In fact, what is good is perhaps and above all the ambiguous, difficult relationship that sets up between languages, proportionately more ambiguous as the languages are numerous, and proportionately more fertile as the relationship is ambiguous.

A.L. Even so, you say that the idea of the constitution of centre is not separable from a centripetal movement. This centripetal movement is thus not separable from a centrifugal movement which is the imaginary projection of the centre upon the world. Consequently, the idea of the centre bears within itself its own contradiction. Would you acquiesce to this paradox?

É.G. No, because generalizing the centre does not comprise bringing in its own contradiction. Contradiction was not at the source of the generalizing intention. The literary problem is translated in these terms: on the interior of this absolute which is the centre, we have seen that the question of legitimization isn't being asked. There is never the need for that. The absolute claims itself as the absolute. The West claims itself as the West, and does not need to justify its action in the world. In the same way, on the inside of this absolute, languages such as English, Spanish, and French vie with each other in their extension over the world without asking the question of their right to absoluteness. In other words, an English writer and a French writer could ignore and even be impervious to each other, and not understand each other: the French didn't understand Shakespeare and proclaimed him a savage; the English didn't understand Racine, murmuring that he produced a literature of weaklings. And neither of them understood German romanticism. This phenomenon extends beyond language, since during the nineteenth century firstcomers in Paris dealt with Beethoven as a vulgar primitive. The French and the English as well could ignore, mistrust, and misunderstand each other. But the question about the absoluteness of language wasn't asked. The absoluteness of the French language remained confirmed for the French just as the absoluteness of the English language remained confirmed for the English: all writers were monolingual. I don't mean that they didn't know other languages, but that when they wrote at their worktable, they were monolingual in the way that they handled their language. They didn't write in the presence of another language, and even less in the presence of all languages. In Europe during the seventeenth, eighteenth, and nineteenth centuries, the case would have been rare if it existed at all. Exceptions might be the Baroque poets of the seventeenth century, Cyrano* and others, who had prescience of the totality-world, and who rose into the Empires of the Sun and the Moon.

A.L. And what about Latinist Chateaubriand, Italianist Stendhal, or Germanist Nerval?**

É.G. Maybe, but I don't think it's certain that these exceptions were important at the time of writing. I am not counting today's writers who speak another language, or who become enamoured of another culture; I am envisioning the writer who, in his own language, using his own language, carries out this practice in the presence of other languages of the world, even if he does not know them. In the past, this process was endogenous everywhere. Endogeny is when literature develops without previous questioning of its legitimization. Today, exogeny is in place.

This is mainly because literatures have been constituted in peripheries, initially in languages of the centre or centres. As a first example I'll cite the literatures of the United States. The entire difference between Henry James and William Faulkner is that James is still inscribed in endogenous literature, whereas Faulkner writes in endo-exogenous literature. In other words, James is still a European in all senses of the term, and Faulkner no longer is, even if he often and eagerly frequents European cultures. Why? It's not only that the United States has 'advanced', a Western nation no longer European,

---

*   Savinien de Cyrano de Bergerac (1619–55) was a French novelist, playwright and poet, linked to the libertine literature of the first half of the seventeenth century. Although there has been a recent resurgence of interest in his work, he is remembered primarily as the inspiration for Edmond Rostand's play *Cyrano de Bergerac* (1897).

**   François-René de Chateaubriand (1768–1848) was a French writer, politician and diplomat who played a foundational role in the Romantic movement in French literature. Marie-Henri Beyle (1783–1842), better known by his pseudonym Stendhal, was a nineteenth-century French writer often considered a Romantic realist. Gérard de Nerval (1808–55) was the pen name of the French writer, poet, and translator Gérard Labrunie, another key figure of French romanticism. As Glissant notes, all three are known for the external influences on their literary production.

a victorious periphery that has become a centre, but because literatures have been formed and constituted in the very dynamic of Western progression, and that then have had repercussions upon centred literatures, or upon literatures which tended toward becoming centred. It's no accident that today, in 1991, in France, South American literatures have just as much currency as French literature, even if this should be only temporary. A normal repercussion which, moreover, has always existed, even in this same French literature: at a certain time Lautréamont came over from Montevideo, the Parnassians emerged from the islands, and Baudelaire translated Edgar Poe. The coloration of marginal ways of thinking also occurred, as witnessed in Gauguin and in the influence of African and Oceanic arts on European arts. An 'exogeneity' is interposed. This is also (and thus) when the writer begins to write in the presence of all of the world's languages. No longer does he write in the presence of his language alone.

There are formal examples, natural or operational, of bilingualism such as we see in Beckett or Nabokov. But there is especially an intervention of works about the structure of language and about the intrusion of all the world's languages, an intervention detectable in works such as Joyce's *Finnegans Wake*, the *Cantos* of Ezra Pound, and already in the *Stèles* of Victor Segalen. In all of these works, exogeneity fundamentally informs endogeny. There are also works born out of the old peripheries, such as the epics of the African griots, works which we already know but which we haven't learned how to integrate. How many Wolof sayings and turns of expression do I have in me, without my being aware of them? There is also the enormous unknown dimension of the corpora of translation, which, I am certain, will gradually come to be recognized as an autonomous and creative art. Of course, we may find remarks such as these everywhere. They are commonplaces dear to me.

This 'exogeneity' extends very far: today, if we consider that literature is engaged with the world, engaged with what I call the Whole-World, well then, we must assume that literature will no longer confer the absoluteness that the certainty of my legitimacy would have provided for me. Instead, and perhaps already, it will bolster the weakness lurking in the adventures of my relativities.

One should be in the Whole-World without giving up on cultivating oneself, on 'knowing how to profit from one's own being', as Montaigne says. So the question of literature is inverted. Being marginal or off-centre is not and would no longer be, in literature, recognizing oneself in a centre and, on the inside of this same centre, uttering the blasphemies that had to be and need to be pronounced (in the full sense of the term, blasphemies), as did Montaigne, Rabelais, the Libertines, Diderot, Rimbaud and Lautréamont, up to Artaud. Neither would it be uttering all the necessary rebukes, as so many authors and so many artists throughout the world have done within the framework of innumerable literatures and cultures which we cannot yet claim to know.

Thinking the ex-centric will no longer amount to uttering masterful blasphemies against an absolute, even if this act entails bringing on the terrors of malediction. Instead, thinking the ex-centric will be about attempting to actualize a relativity without losing oneself in the process, meditating one's own being and cultivating it in relation to all of the world's places. The very dimension of literatures is changed by this.

The absolute is not in the centre, nor elsewhere, but in everything; magnitude is calculable from everywhere, and wandering cures the bad habits of immobility.

A.L. I see very clearly the gist of what you are saying. Still, the part concerning the conservation of identity or even its construction (one can imagine such a case) seems mysterious to me. I understand the relational aspect. I thoroughly understand the multiplication aspect, but the 'construction' of identity is lost on me.

É.G. Here is the issue: if I am not identical to myself, if I don't find in myself the force of my own transformation, I dissociate or am indifferent in relation to everything that is happening in the world. I cut myself off from my own action in the world, I act upon the world, but by denying it. It is all too obvious that this will pose a problem. On the other hand, if I find in the world reasons for my own transformation, I can then be submitted to a phenomenon of creolization which I would no longer control by myself, and this could occur in the very field of my identity. In other words, I could steep myself in the world. Do we need to return to that first concept of identity, according to which perfect identity is the identity of power? Is power over the world constitutive of identity? The connection is worth assuming, because in the same stroke it returns to the issue of the centre and the absolute. The United States is a world-wide power, but as a result, is the identity of its citizens an absolute identity? (Do we conceive of identities as superior to others?) Did Roman identity truly crush the identity of Numidians, Scythians, or Alans? And in another respect, *if I want only to be identical to myself, and identical to myself alone*, which would necessarily occur in isolation and immobilization, then I soon wear myself out simply by existing, alone or in community. Aren't little countries somewhere in the world – in the farthest reaches of a land of fire or a glacial ocean, in the Pacific, or around the Mediterranean, or in Scandinavia, or no matter where – aren't these little countries, without our knowing it, just as constitutive of Relation in the Whole-World, and in just as strong, determinate, and perhaps decisive a manner?

Isn't the question of identity to be linked to a kind of organic function in the Whole-World, a function that is not obvious in light of economic and political or military power? Isn't some sort of ineffable rapport, one that we don't really perceive, being woven now in the 'melting pot', in the mixing. And isn't this rapport changing notions of identity, implying that we are imperceptibly migrating from the old conception of identity as Being to a new conception of identity as Relation?

Inside Relation, aren't there possibilities of regrettable dilution? Considering this, must we fear Relation? All obvious considerations, but which, in fact, are not so obvious. The first of these is that identity, whether personal or collective, is not decreed, but proceeds from a naturalness, and that its mystery is more to be extolled than its definitions. It is, moreover, this last modality which enabled the fascist avatars of identity, and which still maintains them.

A.L. What form might these obvious considerations take in the future? How might we represent them? How might we imagine them?

É.G. We cannot predict that, because we experience Relation as unforeseeable. One of the first approximations that I proposed about the phenomena of creolization is that they are unpredictable. What is apparent in creolization and obvious in Relation is that they are both open, they do not project, they no longer proceed in a defined direction. Since they no longer proceed in a defined direction, you cannot foresee anything about them. You can foresee, if you will, in a projection with a defined direction: it is a privilege which centred mindsets claim or arrogate to themselves. But within a spiral or circularity, you cannot foresee. Circular nomadism obeys necessities which are very close to organic satisfaction and not to any sort of decision or will.

We should perhaps adopt a new 'moral' attitude of thinking, which would entail always being capable of expecting the unexpected. No longer only and always constructing the predictable, as we have done up until now, but also at all times being alert to every unpredictability. Perhaps then we could recognize our obvious considerations. There again, it would require a profound mutation in the mentalities of human beings, an acute mutation of our imaginaries. In the here and now, we can easily recapitulate, in a detailed and precise way, the forms of influences which act upon our imaginaries. But to me, this does not seem decisive. What is interesting to me is a complete opening to unpredictability; in it, we can detect not only a new aesthetic (beauty, the always unexpected beauty of the world), but further still, a new ethic which would result from this aesthetic.

A.L. You have described oracular speech as a paradigm of the speech which channels the energy of the world, a speech which makes it so that man is still one with the world. But isn't it the very nature of language to separate man from the world? Inventing, producing the concept from the very beginning, language separates man from the world. From this perspective, systematic thought does no more than explicate the rational aspect of language, the event of separation which allows us to think the world in terms of linguistic structure.

É.G. No, I don't believe that language initially bears the concept, nor that it initially spreads through it. There are languages of intensity, of affectivity, or languages of contact that do not pass through the concept. Here is our current situation: we have already experienced the concept, meaning that, beginning with Plato, there has already been this separation of man from the world. And for a long time afterwards, this concept has ruled the invaded just as much as the invaders. In my opinion, beginning with the Platonic idea, the pre-Socratic principle of inalienable knowledge was called into question. Plato thus rejects the authority of two principles of knowledge: the inalienable principle of the pre-Socratics, man and the world, and then the fusing principle of the Sophists, completion through language. He questions these two modes of relation to the world to establish what he considers to be the true relation, which is the ideational relation. Confident Aristotelian realisms proceeded from a masterful fantasy such as this.

The ideational relation necessarily ended up at the concept which separates man from the world. The problem is that, today, we are not in a pre-Socratic situation because we bear, whether we want it or know it or not, the historical weight of the concept. This is because most attempts to go back to a poetic knowledge which would not be diffused through the concept have taken and continue to take on the form of a claim: we have to fight against something, specifically, the historical burden of the concept which weighs on us, and this was not the case for the pre-Socratics. Lucky Parmenides, who knew nothing of this fertile torment. Language didn't produce the concept from the beginning, Aristotle was the one who placed it on us. So the situation turns out to be more complicated: our task now is to know if we can simultaneously integrate into a knowledge the inalienable values of the pre-Socratics (which we may roughly resume by saying that they would be the values of the cosmic and the cosmic imaginary), and the principles of rational knowledge that began with Plato and still exist in us. These principles do not integrate the dimensions of the cosmic, the irrational, or the autonomous imaginary, without mentioning any aspiration to be at one with the language. So, in another connection, aren't you astounded that entire cultures, elaborated not so long ago in the margin of Plato's ideational relation, have been universally submitted to the law of the concept?

We are in a new set of circumstances requiring that we be open and naïve, while being learned. And I say open and naïve in the full sense of the terms: we need to be immediate, in contact with the world, and at the same time rational, reflecting about the world. In the history of the Western world, poets have gradually freed themselves from the role of histrion or entertainer that Plato had assigned to them as he drove them out of the City, and have returned to a pre-Socratic aspiration carrying the ambition of a total poetic knowledge. Most of the poets who have done this, and the real example is Rimbaud, are accursed poets. Witness Nietzsche and Artaud. This is because when they launch or risk this effort, rational knowledge has already triumphed, and poetic knowledge appears as a sort of foolish claim. We don't have the courage of their absoluteness, which is all about Relation. The instinctive naïveté of the poet is the semblance behind which he founds his true skill.

Given the positions in which we exist in the world (and not only in the Western world, as many other poetics have come to inscribe themselves on our horizons, specifically the poetics of African countries and of the African diaspora, and the poetics of the Far East), the fact of not confining ourselves in a rational knowledge no longer seems to be a malediction. Instead, in the world-wide panorama, in this sort of Chaos world that we occupy, where interrelations and inextricabilities play out so heatedly, the pathways to clear spaces (and I am not saying pathways to enlightenment) can rise up first of all out of the autonomous imaginary and not be deduced from rational knowledge, even if it involves a brush with derelictions. The new poetics, those coming from countries that have been brought to our awareness, and those which are linked to the unforeseen intelligences of the world, help us with this. And that is an old process.

A.L. The language of affectivity, of contact and exchange, a language which is not submitted to concept and which you have discussed: can we not also organize it in a category like the category of the imaginary?

(*A medieval silence, experienced here and for the first time by the interlocutors, falls over Baton Rouge. It's not for nothing that the question has been asked. The immensely lush foliage of a Louisiana oak, like a felled tree of palavers. The rarefied air raises a melancholy which is initially dream-like. The sun ebbs in its shadows. Should we take note of this? Continue on, without letting ourselves be distracted? And besides, who would notice?*)

É.G. This kind of ordering does not seem right to me, on the one hand because the very object to which this sort of language would apply – the world and connection to the world – is an object which can be rationally known but which escapes systematizing because it is unpredictable. On the other hand, because we can of course imagine a category of the imaginary (imagining the imaginary in all of its classifications is to expand it from within itself), but we cannot conceptualize it: the imaginary cannot be abstracted. If it could be, it would be a malleable object, and it isn't. We can conceive of a totality of the object of the imaginary, but we cannot conceive the pure object of the imaginary as an abstraction: in no way can we conceptualize the imaginary. So, it is in no way a category. We will admit the imaginary as a totalizing dimension of the world. But we can neither admit nor consider it as a concept, precisely because the imaginary escapes all prevision. One of the founding claims of the concept is to include all possibility and, as a result, to authorize prevision. True languages of intuition are in no way constructed out of the totality. If the imaginary can at times be filtered through a maximum of intuition, these two fundamentals always overtake each other.

A.L. The basic epistemological break which keeps us from speaking about the West other than as a phantasm is what I call the Christian epistemological break, when the intervention of the body combines empiricism, abstraction, and concept.

É.G. This Christian epistemological break would be universally valid, but would not be of the West? I think it is the most Western paradigm shift that can be, and I don't believe it is universally established. That is to say, if we don't consider this universal as a division of consensual relations. In other words, we can admit that Christian teleology is universally established, but only from an act of faith, not from a creative and mustering poetic act. With this one reservation, I am in agreement with you about the rest. But the West is not our phantasm, nor yours; it is its own intention unto itself, and in that capacity it continues today to drag us along with it. Surely, that is a desire for eternity. The West does not formally direct present-day globalization, it gives place to it.

I keep on thinking, and this again is a commonplace of knowledge which has not been doubted by any scientific discipline, that the Christian epistemological break exists already in the Platonic text. First of all, when Plato affirms that eternal ideas exist in an empyrean which is a prefiguration of Christian paradise; next, when he considers that the soul falls into the body and that the body is the tomb of the soul, prefiguring notions of sin and resurrection; and finally, when he projects that knowledge can be accomplished only through working up by degrees, a sort of asceticism of the entire being, through a contemplation of the Beautiful, the True and the Good. These all seem to me to be principles examined by Christian epistemology: a redemptive beyond, the mystery of the duality of body and soul, and elevation as the pathway to knowledge.

It is no surprise that Christian churches initially admitted and considered Plato as a precursor. I don't believe that the Christian epistemological break contributes any real or appreciable differentiation in relation to Platonic thought on these points. The Church, once established as an institution, will reclaim the concept to combine it with its mysteries. Plato is at the source of the redeeming universal, and pre-Socratic poets had displayed multiplicity.

What we can maintain here is that the Christian break generalizes, or universalizes, the possibility for each individual to attain knowledge, which was not given in the Platonic theme. In the Platonic theme, not just anyone could be a philosopher. There is a division of tasks in the city, with people who work, others who guard and protect, but it is the philosopher-kings who direct: the only ones who have attained true knowledge. Crypto-Prosperos before the fact. Another commonplace.

What Christian thought adds is a manner of democratization, inasmuch as it trivializes this position. In other words, it makes it possible for every individual to be a philosopher-king. Transcendence can thus be shared. Theories of grace will later lend nuance to this project, specifically in discussing the apportioning of the elected and their merit before their god. But aside from this, the collective mind, which was not really learned, does not really notice any leap in thinking.

A.L. I see what you mean in that the Church was for a long time Neoplatonic, through Saint Augustine, and then, Aristotelian because of Saint Thomas. However, I would propose this paradox: during these two great moments of its philosophy, the Church is anti-Christian. Why? Because, if you will, for Aristotle and Plato alike, you have mentioned the empyrean, according to which the divine form of the idea always remains in an eternal fixed heaven. With the incarnation, however, God becomes a man, meaning that he is integrated like and as a god into human history. If the divine idea is not kept, regardless of faith, we do not see the necessity or importance of the Christian break in relation to a tradition of celestial spheres, in which gods have very little to do directly with the history of man. With the incarnation, the concept of the divine becomes historical.

É.G. Let's still not leave the last word to this humanization of the divine. Let's develop one of those other silences that we have detected in the Middle Ages, silences which are extended, deepened, and perpetuated between two repressions of heretics, in the terrifying decelerations of a Hundred Years' War, after the rampages of a peasant revolt, on the morning of a learned woman's torture or the torment of a soothsayer. Let's ask ourselves if this systematic thought, which no longer produces splendours, hasn't begun to filter here and there inspirations from the ideas of elsewhere and the other into new regimes of oppression and ignorance? Will it be the same for the deafening silences that henceforth accompany our wanderings in the world? Will we hear the promise of oral poets, will we understand the intense fire of convergent writings, along with the countries and landscapes which they lift and compose? Will we raise up our worldly states?

This long twilight, which has masked the defeat of the thoughts of the multiplicity in the European Middle Ages, fell like a curtain over a stage. Learned men, staunchly armed with the *Summa* of Saint Thomas, will remain intransigent, conceding nothing, not even to the Neoplatonics. Wars of Religion will settle it once and for all, and from then on all these cultures will prepare for the solemn council and confiscation without recourse of the world and its marvels.

Let us now reflect, and we'll be in agreement on this, upon the evermore difficult humanization of the humanities, striving to endure in their diversities, the unexpected, the blended, the inextricable.

Spumes, the Day After

You find in fact, in the folds of the world's histories, that property has here and there its own nobleness, as well as its own obstinacies or bewildering pillages.

We have chased after a simply liveable idea of love, tried to grub it out from so many disturbances, in bodies, and so many torments, in dreams, *outside the Plantation*: which makes it so that love has often concocted for us a bitter potion in sweet syrup, we would like to drink of it along the way, without stopping, but in all truth, it was also like a curdling, leaving us stunned by the wayside of the path of Sighs.

*Bitter love**

We try each time to close up our houses, our reefs with spumes to make sure that we can fit in.

Whatever is obscure in the story is what moves us, our bodies are immobile.

---

* Glissant uses the expression *le fiel'amour*, making an inverted reference to *le fin'amor*, the code of courtly love initiated by the Provençal troubadours and propagated throughout medieval Europe in poetry and prose romance.

Other peoples have frequented these Gehennas, other landscapes. Their cries go into us.

Countries leave you with: words to scale, heaped stones, naked sufferings.

'Corolla we beg you
'Don't go near the blaze.'

É.G.

November 2007

Alexandre Leupin

The Mangrove Work

I am choosing to assemble the opus (which is diffracted into all genres: poetry, theatre, novel, essay) under the symbolic figure of a tree, a nation-tree, the mangrove. A pioneering and tentacular plant which mixes in with others, the mangrove inaugurates land on maritime salinity, on Martinique, in the Caribbean, in Florida, and Brazil (in the Plantation space), pressing its roots into the sand from the trunk. It is poignant to see the plants throwing their offshoots toward the coast, upon the shoals, with a deceptive fragility and precariousness. Soon an island, an archipelago emerges where there was nothing before but a sea surface shattered by mists, and every hurricane is defied with a preliminary patience.

For Glissant brought himself to life in his archipelago-writing by virtue of a grounding decision, a gesture, a courage, to practice his writing where no model had previously colonized literary territory. The person who actually reduces this work to an ensemble of external determinations (slavery, misery, the colony, influences) will see nothing of it: Glissant lives by being detached from any environment – in order to return to it and manifest it better --, miming the original tearing away from the native soil of Africa suffered by ancestral slaves, in blood and terror. To designate what had lost its origin, it was necessary to be cut off from the lost origin. This was the price for the power of nomination.

And now names shimmer, spread through prodigious and lush foliages, 'names arise, not magnified in memory by those one hundred fifty years fallen into the chasm, but as if engendered by the slope, or maybe secreted in the hole of the world's silent eye, or gushing forth from the bottomless well where the ball and chain turn into pearls in the entrails of the drowned' (Malemort).*

There was no longer a legitimate father, and consequently, no son or daughter either: 'He asked you who your father was, and the father of your father up to the seventh line, and not one could respond, not one could say here is my descendant and the descendant of my descendant up until this land turns into rottenness and fertility...' (Malemort) It will be necessary to dream one up, a first ancestor, and this will be the rebellious slave 'Odono, disembarked in 1715' (Mahogany),** who himself was the forerunner of the first runaway slave, Papa Longoué of The Fourth Century.*** Odono, whose patronym endows with meaning, and possibly confers fertilities, is also a question mark who morally torments every genealogy.

---

* *Malemort* (Violent Death) is a 1975 novel by Glissant set in Martinique.
** *Mahogany* is a 1987 novel by Glissant, recounting the stories of several maroons in Martinique across the nineteenth and twentieth centuries.
*** *The Fourth Century* is a 1964 novel by Glissant that recounts the search by a young Mathieu Béluse to discover the lost history of his country, Martinique.

There were no more villages, landscapes, families; there were only the cabins of the Habitation wretchedly granted by the master. The individual will be invented out of that, through and in spite of the pain and munificence of being a slave, through and in spite of the tenure and horror of being a master: and then, in a paradox and turnaround, the cabin becomes the commander's.

There was no longer any 'time from Before': it will be dreamed, more just and precise than in any lost archive in the shoddy functioning of an administration. With an equal focus on denouncing subsidized alienation and clearing away from it, outside of place and in place, the new spaces of the Whole-World will be inaugurated, where in another Babel, the stammered vocables of every island-language will be exchanged.

There was a great discourse, of Aimé Césaire and others. It was necessary to invent other names, to rewrite and reutter all names. Then, all of a sudden, the defeats of living turn inside out like a glove, in the pleasure of writing; in this regard, there is no gesture more loaded with optimism than Glissant's writing. Through the execution of the work, he proves the possible infinity of a speech that transcends its limits, and he makes a gift of it to others who are to come.

The tenants of the 'homeland' and of everything that is called realism (socialist?) incessantly rebuked the texts for their obscurity: they would have liked to read in them a more straightforward reproduction of a Martinican reality, a denunciation of the oppressor, an exaltation of the victim, and the picturesque holding hands with a universalizing and assimilating humanism. Instead of that, they find an opacity claimed as such, a pathway toward otherworldly Being that escapes all naming, a virtuosity of language found in Proust, Céline or Faulkner (a double and American brother who produced the deepest figures of the plantation world, analyzed in Faulkner, Mississippi,* *a work by the same author of* The Ripening*), and a stupefying 'creole' syntax which renews our grammatical habits from top to bottom. We cannot say it enough: 'French' literature always recharges itself from an operation on syntax —Montaigne, Racine, Céline — rather than upon the lexicon, even if in Glissant creole names are sometimes called into a joyous baroque copulation with those from France.*

'Understanding possibly in the future that we needed to hear: change the word! And without trembling or caesura take up the new language –which?— and with grief and sweat and pain and in drunken descent fling its syntax into

---

* *Faulkner, Mississippi* is a 1996 essay by Glissant, written during his time at Louisiana State University in Baton Rouge, in which he provides a deeply personal interpretation of the American author.

the grasses on both sides' (Malemort). *They are in there, the descendants of tradition, a theory and poetic practice which together equal, sometimes through confrontation, those of the greatest writers.*

It's actually that which bothers us, this obstinate refusal to work in local colour, in wretched confinement, in a realist rut or expansive exoticism; this tearing away from all determinations, excepting those of the poetic languages presented; this attention directed toward the gesture of writing (and here there is no prim formalism so dear to universities, but something more complex and monstrously vital); this assumed murk which multiplies one hundred-fold the possibilities of language and the most subtle resources for the unsettling of our Being.

Impossible to sort out the idiom; academics are disconcerted by it. Glissant shows a completely different path, unclassifiable. Every revolt takes place through the grandeur of a new language, and nothing is more disturbing for the false superiority of the old colonizer than the absolute mastery of artistic means put to work, than the tranquil assurance of a high style which is an implicit criticism of all conventional language. Never reducible if not to its own light and shade, the work is because of that a figure of subversion. In this way, it can only be taught through misunderstanding: addressed to readers that it creates by degrees with its progression, it challenges the officialdom of disciples and the scholarly stamping of critics, to take us one by one, by the throat, by the stomach, by the head like a great boiling fever. All convenient categories, national literature, and 'French' clarity of dull common sense, persecuted whimpering, and dissent when it is only an aspiration to take the accursed place of the political master, are dismissed without compromise.

There are no characters here; landscapes supplant them, described with minutiae in their rhetorical efflorescence. Characters are only assumed and defined by their voices, established poets in their particularity, only by obscure gestures of approbation or refusal. Similar to the novelist, the people of his work are designated by a manner of speaking which is well above the necessities of communication. What is evoked in them is the obsessional pleasure of making oneself exist through poetry. But such an insistence upon expression is in no way an illusion, poetic reverie, or otherworldly flight into phantasm. Instead, Glissant shows that, to exist, worlds must be named. If not, there will be no 'poetics of Relation', nor any plunge into the diverse. In this regard, Glissant is for me the successor of the great logothetes of Western tradition, beginning with those of the Old Testament who always knew not only that utterance was inaugural, but further, that its legitimacy could only be found in a poetics.

What Glissant brought about in the name of 'creolization' provides here both theory and practice, absolutely inseparable. But what must be understood by 'creole'? First of all, an entirely separate language, with its particular grammar and syntax, unlike any others. Then, a language which has the vitality to create itself in a very short time span (we may think of the vernacular languages of the Middle Ages), and suddenly form a community. Out of this birth-creation situated at the crossroads of several cultures, Glissant traces the necessity of putting all the languages of the world in relation (Introduction to a Poetics of Diversity).* Creolization is the clashing, with unforeseeable results, of all the cultures between themselves, a collision made possible by the globalization of communication. In optimism and utopian generosity, Glissant proposes a conversation between languages in which none of them has a privileged position, in which reciprocal exchanges endlessly create newness, without its place calculated in advance. According to him, this is what distinguishes creolization from hybridism, whose results can be projected: 'But this exploding sea, and all the islands of the world, are creole, or in other words, unforeseeable. And all the continents, whose shores are incalculable' (Whole-World).** So then Being has to be defined out of a practice of exchange, of cultures rubbing up against each other, out of a poetics that never stops being sure of itself: 'To speak to the world, try out a language of sparks, driven onto the seas like a creel of silver' (Malemort). All languages are capable of truths: 'In any given language, creating thus supposes that one be inhabited by the impossible desire of all languages in the world. Totality hails us. Every work of literature today is inspired by it' (Poetics of Relation).***

We recall those troubadours of the twelfth century, who rubbed their language up against others: Raimbaut d'Orange, mixing Latin and Provençal, Raimbaut de Vaqueiras (Provençal, Italian, French, Gascon, and Gallo-Portuguese);**** the foundational texts of French literature, which create ex nihilo the nobility of a poetic writing out of a serf language, which is what Old French was in its beginnings. Couldn't the same be said of the setting for the appearance of French Creole languages in the Caribbean? We also think, later, about Montaigne, who defined himself as 'a hybrid, my ass between two chairs'. Just as much as

---

* *Introduction to a Poetics of Diversity* is a 1996 volume in which Glissant sets out his key ideas in a manner more pedagogical than many of his other writings.
** *Whole-World* is a 1993 novel by Glissant in which he explores his view of the world as a network of interrelated cultures and communities, the contact between which leads to dynamic and shifting cultural formations.
*** *Poetics of Relation* is a 1990 collection of essays by Glissant – the third volume of his *Poétique* [Poetics] series – in which he sets out his key ideas on the concept in the title central to his reflection on cultural interconnections.
**** Raimbaut of Orange (c.1147–73) and Raimbaut de Vaqueiras or Vaqueyras (1180–1207) were both Provençal troubadours.

these great foundational authors, Glissant poetically resurrects the possibility of a speech in all directions.

I will conclude here with a misgiving: the motif of all, the relativism of all cultures, even if they do not proceed here from a half-baked and formulaic multiculturalism, still provoke the same anxieties in the reader. It is not that Glissant ignores the suffering and the violence of the world, but, first of all, because 'nothing is everything': the project of embracing the totality of beings arises perhaps from the discourse of the master (Hegel), and all of history has taught us to be suspicious of it. Next, because supposing the dialogue of the Whole-World, the copresence of all languages to each other, is perhaps getting tripped up, through optimism and nobility, about the respective tolerance of cultures. When there is no authority to transcend old particularities, murders arise, provoked by the narcissism of 'a little difference', class and race genocides so widely practiced in the twentieth century – an historical avatar not reserved to the West alone. This approach thus ends with a question mark, addressed to one of our greatest living writers, one of those who are the most important to us at the beginning of this millennium.

November 2000

9781789621303